DECK & PATIO

STYLES

CHRISTINA NELSON

CONSULTANT: JOSEPH R. CARTER

PUBLICATIONS INTERNATIONAL, LTD.

Louis Weber, C.E.O.
Publications International, Ltd.
7373 North Cicero Avenue
Lincolnwood, Illinois 60646

8 7 6 5 4 3 2 1

ISBN: 0-7853-1305-2

Library of Congress Catalogue Card Number: 95-72996

CONTRIBUTING WRITER: CHRISTINA NELSON

CONSULTANT: JOSEPH R. CARTER

Christina Nelson is a former editor at *Home* magazine who has concentrated her writing on subjects relating to the home, architecture, design, and landscaping. Her work has appeared in *American Home Style*, *Custom Builder*, *Decorating-Remodeling*, *Home Mechanix*, and *New Home*.

Joseph R. Carter is former editor-in-chief of *Home Owner* magazine and has worked as a consultant, editor, and writer on home-related topics for over twenty years. He has contributed to numerous publications including *Build It!*, *Family Home*, and *Wood Beautiful*.

CONTENTS

INTRODUCTION

An attractive, functional outdoor living area can be one of the finest features of a home, enhancing its appearance, increasing livability, and bringing pleasure to those who use the space. As more and more people retreat to the home to seek relief from the fast pace of the times, decks and patios are becoming preferred places to relax after work, entertain friends, and regroup with the family. Given the right amenities, decks and patios can even become substitutes

for the weekend getaway—the swimming pool supplanting a crowded beach, and the built-in barbecue taking over the picnic in the park.

Whether a new or improved outdoor area calls for a deck or patio depends on several factors: the site itself, the style and size of the house, individual lifestyle and

personal preferences, and budget. And though the site may

be the deciding factor in choosing between a deck and a

patio and the budget may determine the number of amenities

that can be included, other less

tangible aspects should be addressed as well.

Taking stock of one's lifestyle is a good place to begin.

Who will use the area and how many functions is it

expected to fulfill? Will the space

serve primarily as a transition zone between house and yard, or

will it double as an indoor-outdoor room? Will the setting be

casual or formal, a quiet retreat, or the hub of activity? A family

composed of toddlers, teens, pets, and parents

probably requires a different design from that of a

couple who like to relax on their own or entertain

on a small scale. Personal taste is also an important

matter to consider when planning an outdoor area—

whether it's a preference for a certain color stone on the

patio floor or a particular style of railing for the deck.

Typically though, the actual

site will have a greater effect on

the end result than anything else. It can provide

opportunities for creative solutions to challenging conditions.

An outdoor area has to respond to the lay of the land, but it

should also balance the amount of sun and shade. Structures such as trees and shrubbery, trellises, or privacy walls can increase outdoor comfort by moderating the sun, shielding the area from prevailing winds, and screening out unwanted sights and sounds.

A successful deck or patio, however, is much more than a response to particular location or need. A well-designed deck or patio integrates diverse elements into a functional and

aesthetically pleasing whole that harmonizes with the house it serves and the yard it adjoins. For instance, materials don't have to match the house facade exactly, but they should complement it in style and

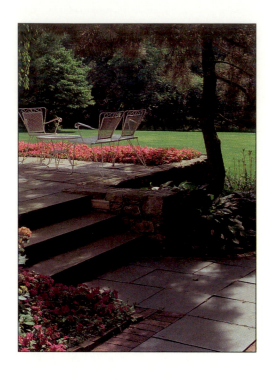

mood. Perhaps the ideal design for a traditional brick-face home would be a new brick patio, but a sloping site makes a patio an impractical choice. One solution could be a series of wood platforms connected by brick steps that descend to a brick walkway. The idea is to create a unified appearance that is balanced with a variety of colors, forms, and textures to add interest and offset monotony.

A successful patio or deck also remains in scale with the house and the surrounding landscape. A small outdoor area usually looks better with a simple,

uncluttered design. By contrast, a big yard may call for a large outdoor area to keep things in proportion, but the overall space can be divided or sectioned with a change in levels, contrasting

materials, or garden accents.

The following pages offer a wide sampling of deck

and patio styles to serve as inspiration for developing

and planning outdoor living spaces. A portfolio of ideas rather

than a how-to manual, this book discusses basic deck types

and presents a number of deck styles for both contemporary

and traditional homes. It covers a large variety of patio

materials and looks at some of the ways they can be used.

Finally, it describes some of the amenities and finishing

touches that can make both decks and patios more

functional, enjoyable outdoor spaces.

DESIGNS TO SUIT A SITE

Because of their design flexibility, decks can be made to respond to a wide variety of site conditions. They can hug the ground or rise high above it; they can flatten a steep slope with a single platform or conform to its contours with multiple levels; or they can lie close to a house or stand apart on their own. Decks can even fit on the rooftop or stretch out from an upper-story wall.

Deciding which deck design best suits a house and its surroundings requires some careful thought and planning. It means looking at practical matters such as the actual lay of the land, areas of sun and shade, wind direction, and privacy. A challenging site might require professional assistance to help with design and construction.

A successful deck design considers the aesthetics of the site as well, fitting in with the house and its existing landscape. With a little ingenuity, natural features such as boulders or trees can be treated as assets rather than obstacles and focal points rather than distractions. A good design will allow the shape and size of the deck to suit a range of activities associated with outdoor living.

THREE-PART HARMONY

Beautifully integrated with its surroundings, this understated redwood deck (right) floats at the edge of a swimming pool. Designed in three sections, the deck sports a middle platform that serves as a bridge connecting the tiled walkway and entry deck to the secluded sitting area beyond.

ATTACHED DECKS EASE TRANSITIONS

SHADED PRIVACY

Private and protected, this welcoming entry deck (below) beckons visitors to pause at the bench en route to the front door. The narrow floor boards and slatted trellis contrast nicely with the diagonal pattern of the roughly sawn siding. Design: John Herbst, Jr.

Connected to the house at the front, back, or even the side, attached decks ease the transition from interior spaces to the outdoors in several ways. They permit ready access in both directions and allow the deck to serve as another living area. When the deck lies at or near the same level as the interior floor, it becomes a natural extension of the room inside, especially if the spaces are separated by sliding glass or French doors. When accessed from several rooms, an attached deck can become a multifunctional area ideal for entertaining, dining, gardening, or relaxing.

By nature of their role as transition areas between street and home, entry decks often have a more formal appearance than those at the back or side of the house. Decks that lie just off informal living spaces, such as the kitchen or family room, nearly always adopt a more casual air.

CLASSICAL COLUMNS

Classical detailing and classic simplicity turn this front entrance deck (right) into an architectural statement. The unobtrusive path, the spare landscape, and the deck's low profile focus attention on the pergola-topped columns and deep-sheltered entry. Design: Todd Soli Architects.

BEACHFRONT BEAUTY

This shingled beach house (right) features a curving second-story balcony-deck that opens the master bedroom to natural light and stunning water views. The deck also offers a recessed sitting area tucked away from neighbors' sight. The lower deck exhibits the same gentle radius form. Design: Todd Soli Architects.

BALCONY RETREATS ALLOW PRIVACY

Whether they offer intimate glimpses of the garden below or broader vistas of the landscape beyond, balconies and balcony-decks can be incorporated into almost any home design. They can suit virtually any site because they sit well above the ground, unaffected by terrain, and can be added to an existing house with a minimum of fuss. Typically reached only from an interior room, they serve especially well as private retreats.

Traditionally, balconies projected outward from buildings only as far as the roof above and were contained by partial walls and substantial railings. More contemporary-minded balcony-decks, on the other hand, often extend a distance from the house, making room for close-in areas of privacy and shade and farther out, less sheltered areas open to the sun and sky. Either way, balconies can be most welcome as airy yet protected extensions of interior spaces.

CURVES AHEAD

Strikingly contemporary in design, this front entry (above) follows a traditional formula by extending out just as far as the line of the roof. Above the entry, a balcony-deck subtly integrates the privacy and shelter of a roofed enclosure with a dramatic curved extension open to its surroundings.
Design: Mojo-Stumer Architects.

A COZY RETREAT

This charming semicircular balcony (right) feels cozy and quaint, thanks to a railing that has the appearance of an old-fashioned fence. A petite retreat, it's just large enough for a small table and chair, and it makes a perfect spot for enjoying a good book or a cup of coffee.

FOLLOWING THE SITE, UP OR DOWN

Steep up and down slopes are a little more difficult to tame than gentler ones, and multiple levels are one of the best solutions. Design- and construction-wise, gradually stepping levels up or down an incline is practical, visually exciting, and more in keeping with the natural setting. Since most houses are built at the top of a slope rather than at its base, most decks tend to start on high and proceed downward, sometimes as a straightforward split-level, often as a cascade of several platforms. Of course, many homes lend themselves to a single high-level deck, perhaps cantilevered over a hillside. High decks can present problems, though, especially if they're large. They can overshadow rooms below, and when seen from the bottom of the slope, they may dominate the house itself.

Steep terrain usually dictates a hefty understructure designed to withstand a variety of soil conditions as well as to support the deck. Hiding those underpinnings from view with latticework, siding, or even shrubs can give the deck and your home a more finished appearance.

WOODSY WATERFALL

This secluded bi-level deck in the midst of the woods (right) is separated from the house yet easily accessed from the side. The exposed aggregate surface of the upper pool area complements the natural stone retaining wall and waterfall just below. Edged by cedar decking and concealed with latticework, the lower pool rises 12 feet above grade at the slope base. Design and construction: St. Louis Pool Company.

ON-GRADE DECKS HUG THE GROUND

If your site is level or just slightly sloped, an on-grade deck may be the perfect solution. Whether attached to the house or freestanding, on-grade decks are relatively easy to design and construct. They can be sized and shaped in countless ways. Because they rest fairly close to the ground, they seldom require railings or steps. On-grade decks are especially appropriate additions to single-story homes or to those with a low profile where a raised or multilevel deck might look out of place or overwhelm the existing structure.

Some on-grade decks are designed to sit flush with the ground, but their direct contact with the earth calls for materials that are impervious to decay, such as pressure-treated lumber or a non-wood product such as PVC (polyvinyl chloride) vinyl. Most designs are elevated slightly above the surface of the ground, however, to compensate for uneven or sloping ground and to allow for proper drainage and air circulation.

OUTDOOR LIVING

Stretching along the rear facade, this spacious deck (right) offers a comfortable mix of sun and shade and serves as a versatile multipurpose outdoor room with areas for cooking, dining, and relaxing. Cheerful flower boxes and potted plants dress up the area and help break up the expanse. Pressure-treated lumber: Wolmanized Lumber.

PRACTICAL STYLE

A charming white fence echoes the house trim and creates an airy sitting and dining enclosure for this cozy on-grade deck (left). Set on a bed of crushed stone, which complements the exterior brick, the PVC vinyl decking offers a low-maintenance alternative to traditional wood. The stone bed also promotes good drainage and helps level the uneven ground. PVC decking: Heritage Vinyl Products.

DECKS THAT SET THEMSELVES APART

Whether the focal point of the yard or simply a highlight in the existing landscape, freestanding decks are yet another way to gain outdoor living space. They can be welcome additions when the house configuration precludes an attached deck or when the ideal location—a grove of trees, near a stream, or overlooking a garden—is some distance away. A freestanding deck is an ideal way to dress up a drab, previously ignored corner of the yard by transforming it into a secluded retreat for reading, a lively play area for children, or a stage for displaying colorful pottery and plants.

Although the term freestanding may suggest a flimsy or temporary solution, stand-alone decks are usually permanent fixtures that adhere to the same structural requirements as other deck types. A design may be as simple as a low-level platform floating just above the ground or as complex as a multilevel system of platforms and connectors that climb up or down a slope or stretch across the yard. Plain or fancy, however, detached decks can offer outdoor living at its best.

LAKESIDE LUXURY

A distance from the house, this multilevel deck (left) blends serenely with its tranquil setting. Its arresting angled design follows the contour of the shoreline. The narrow entrance from the small platform is suggestive of a door leading into a room; on the upper level, a wider opening signals a stairway down to the water's edge. Design: Deck Designs, Inc.

A SUNNY SEAT

A secluded area off the patio makes an ideal spot for this freestanding deck (right). It's a focal point within the symmetrical landscape plan yet understated in its own design. The clean lines of the seat and floorboards balance nicely with the herringbone pattern of the brick walkway. Design: The Brickman Group.

STANDING FREE, BUT FITTING IN

Freestanding decks work especially well as companions to other outdoor elements, such as patios or landscaping, because their materials and designs can be easily tailored to blend or contrast with others. Wood decks lend themselves beautifully to combinations with many types of masonry and stone found in patio construction, such as brick, flagstone, and crushed rock. When colors, shapes, and textures harmonize, the deck and its immediate surroundings often become a unified outdoor space, each flowing into the other. Contrasts, on the other hand, can be used to set the different areas apart and help delineate activities. Here the deck might fit comfortably into the overall landscape plan but intentionally contrast with the nearby lawn or a more distant patio.

As extensions of the home, detached decks should have some connection with the house itself, be it an informal gravel or bark path, a more formal walkway, or a bridge or platform. In a large yard or remote location, a freestanding deck may not be in the direct line of sight of the house, but it should feel like it's just an arm's length away.

IDEAL FOR ENTERTAINING

Compact and self-contained, this well-equipped redwood deck with spa (left) occupies a portion of the backyard that was previously seldom used. The low-level deck, measuring about 23×23 feet, is perfect for entertaining—day or night. It features a wet bar with easy-care tile counters, post lamps controlled from the house, and benches and tables built into the perimeter. Design and construction: John Hemingway.

LEVELS OFFER SITE SOLUTIONS

Many dilemmas associated with outdoor living can be resolved with multilevel decks. They can step up or down a steep or rocky slope to transform an impossible site into a useful one. They might be shaped into a progression of space-saving platforms to make the most of an awkward or cramped outdoor area or arranged in a succession of broader levels to give a large uninteresting yard a new focus. By adding built-in seating, planters, places for sun and shade, and perhaps even a water feature, multilevel decks can become more popular living spaces than the rooms indoors.

All decks look their best when they have a unified appearance. Multiple decks in particular can seem uncomfortably busy if they lack continuity in materials or design. Repeating a railing detail, platform shape, or bench style will help tie the various levels together.

EMBRACING NATURE

A sideyard that suffered from irregular terrain was put to good use with a pair of simply styled yet multi-functional decks (above), which are oriented to downhill and distant views. Rather than stop short of the stately tree, the lower deck wraps around it, gaining extra space and plenty of shade. Benches on both levels echo the angled railings. Design: Deck Designs, Inc.

WARM UP THE NIGHT

Weathered to a silvery finish, this deck (left) relies on a series of landings and stairs to carry foot traffic down to the outdoor dining and barbecue levels, as well as to the backyard. Wide, angled benches help contain the two lower sections. The large firepit can add a special warmth to nighttime and cool-weather entertaining. Design: Deck Designs, Inc.

LEVELS OF COMFORT

What prettier place than a clearing in the forest for this multileveled, multifaceted wood deck system (right). A pleasing juxtaposition of heights and shapes creates visual interest and helps define the different areas of activity. Ground-level seating tucked in the shadows of the uppermost deck offers relief from the sunnier regions around the spa. Pressure-treated lumber: Wolmanized Lumber.

ENHANCING THE HOME WITH LEVELS

An integral part of this home's design, the deck's descending levels (left) exhibit the same contemporary styling, color palette, and aesthetics as the house itself. The plexiglass cutouts in the main deck railing allow unobstructed views of the yard below. Design: Peter C. Kurth Office of Architecture and Planning.

Multilevel decks aren't always employed to solve site problems; often they serve as enhancements to both house and garden. Frequently, multiple levels are designed as an integral part of a home's architecture to extend the building into the natural surroundings in a gradual and pleasing way. Sometimes they set the stage for a particular style of landscaping or act as bridges or connectors within the landscape. A very large deck has a warmer appearance when broken into levels and is usually in better proportion to the scale of the house. Built-in planters and seating can be incorporated to help signal a change in levels, and if positioned properly, they can even take the place of conventional rails. Multiple decks also lend themselves to interesting patterns that can be repeated on other levels—changing the direction of the floorboards on steps, for instance, shaping corners on the diagonal, or implementing horizontal railings rather than traditional vertical designs.

The rather reserved demeanor of this house and its adjoining decks (right) is balanced by a lively landscape consisting of raised beds and containers filled with flowers and greenery. The bi-level deck design, subdued in color only, also displays a lively mix of line and form that complements the house, the plantings, and the garden structure. Design: The Brickman Group.

RAISED DECKS FLOAT ABOVE GRADE

For a house that's built on a virtually level site, gaining an out-door living area can be a relatively simple matter; an on-grade deck that lies flush with the ground or a concrete or stone patio can be just the answer. But few sites are perfectly flat, and the solution invariably calls for a deck that's raised off the ground on a system of posts. The term "raised" is rather broad since it encompasses nearly all types of decks that are not built directly on the ground. A raised deck can float a foot or so above grade—perhaps just enough to bring the deck floor up to the same level as the threshold of the back door. Or it might extend several feet from the ground to be on the same level as interior rooms, then gradually step its way down a slope. A raised deck can be a free-standing structure out in the yard or a wraparound element attached directly to the house.

Decks built close to the ground usually require a rela-tively simple support system. More expansive or compli-cated decks, as well as those that sit above the ground, demand a substructure engi-neered for stability and bear-ing loads.

SIMPLE PLEASURES

Raised to meet the level of interior rooms, this simple deck (below) seems to float above the ground. The short distance between deck and yard permits a low benchlike railing to serve as a safety barrier. Patio doors: Morgan Manufacturing.

SWEEPING STAIRWAYS

Redwood decks and a new screened-in porch (right) update a turn-of-the-century home for modern living while blending harmoniously with its Victorian style and mood. The raised semicircular deck adds visual interest and helps soften the rather imposing rear facade. A pair of curved stairs hugging the bow of the deck descend to the sloping yard. The latticework provides an element of design. Design: Bowie Gridley Architects.

EXPAND HORIZONS FROM THE ROOF

With a little imagination and the right type of roof, a rooftop deck can offer a penthouse view of the world and a refreshing new outlook on outdoor living. Roof decks are especially welcome where outside sitting areas are minimal or nonexistent, a particular concern in many city locations and condominium complexes. A roof deck can also serve as an ideal vantage point to capture distant vistas and watch the sun slip below the horizon or the moon rise. Many older homes in coastal locations, especially those built before the turn of the century, were constructed with a widow's walk or similar roof deck to facilitate watching for the return of ships or the arrival of storms.

Naturally, rooftop decks are most easily added where the roof surface is flat or only slightly pitched and where there is easy access to the area by an exterior staircase, perhaps, or through an upper-story window that's been converted to a door. A roof with a slope will probably require a building professional to assist with deck construction. Safety, of course, is also an issue, so railings and half-walls should be sturdy and secure.

SEAWORTHY STYLE

A nautical mood pervades this rooftop deck (left), reminiscent of the widow's walk that graced so many seaside homes of yesteryear. The crisp design and spiral staircase ascending from the second-story deck inject a modern note. Landscape design: Ivy Reid.

CITY GARDEN

City living takes on a new perspective from this garden oasis atop the roof (right). Designed to make every inch count, the rooftop deck offers sun and shade, color and fragrance—not to mention cut flowers—and, most of all, a private retreat away from it all.

OUTDOOR LIVING OVER THE GARAGE

Decks can adapt to a whole range of locations—even the roof of a garage. Overlooked but often ideally proportioned and sized to accommodate a roomy deck, a flat-roof garage can be simply and inexpensively outfitted with a floor and railings. Whether the garage is detached or connected to the house, it can usually accept an exterior staircase and may even lend itself to a second-story bridge. Carports with a strong roof system have great possibilities as well. Garages topped with gently sloped or gabled roofs can also be considered for conversion. Be certain, though, to seek professional help to assure that the deck addition is properly integrated into the house design and safely constructed.

Garage decks, like their rooftop cousins, can be just the answer to a pint-size yard with no room to stretch out or a zero lot-line house with basically no yard space to spare. The deck can feel a bit like a yard when "container landscaped" with small trees, potted shrubs, and planter boxes attached to the railings. Rounded out with some comfortable furnishings, the area becomes a relaxing retreat above it all.

BUILD YOUR OWN BACKYARD

A single-car garage at the rear of this older home was expanded into an oversize garage and given an ample 26×32-foot deck across its roof (left). Accessible from the kitchen and dining room through a quartet of French doors, the second-story deck gives the family an outdoor living space their yard couldn't provide. A sturdy lattice rail safely contains children and pets yet has a light and airy look. Design and construction: Potter Construction.

STYLED TO SUIT THE HOME

A successful deck does more than suit its site and provide outdoor living space. The key to the success of any deck design is that it reflects the character of the house—the architectural style, shape, detailing, and color. The idea is not to copy every aspect but rather to create an overall design that complements and enhances the house and its surroundings.

Although the enjoyment of the outdoors close to the home has been part of leisure activities for years, outdoor living on the deck is a relatively new concept. Decks and patios began appearing in the 1950s attached to the then popular Cape Cod and Western ranch homes. A decade later, with the arrival of the ubiquitous split-level, decks were being incorporated into both modest tract homes and custom designs and soon became a common feature of contemporary American houses everywhere.

This chapter explores the many possibilities among deck styles, including classic designs that complement most homes, new and old. The chapter features a variety of contemporary styles—some created to match the drama of modern architecture with others designed to add zest to plain homes.

DRAMATIC BEAUTY

This breathtaking site (right) called for a classic deck design that was secure and in sync with the natural setting. An unsurpassed lookout for enjoying ocean drama, the unpretentious, weathered deck also integrates well with a nearby lawn area. Together they offer attractive, functional outdoor living spaces on mostly unusable terrain.

CONTEMPORARY DRAMA IN A DECK

Contemporary homes often express a visual drama that's lacking in more traditional styles. Intentionally devoid of ornament and frills, many contemporary designs focus instead on integrating line and form into striking compositions.

In this design—an architect's own home—strong vertical and horizontal surfaces are softened by a curving wall, which is echoed in the curve of the midlevel deck and handrails. The fluid lines of the metal railings carry a nautical theme inspired by a pond that sits near the base of the deck. The open framework of the metal rails and the clear plexiglass inserts of the upper deck wall allow unobstructed views of the surrounding trees and vegetation whether sitting, dining, or soaking in the spa. The plexiglass also serves as a safety measure, keeping children and their toys safely contained. The nautical theme also influenced the color scheme of the house and deck design—a driftwood gray on walls, a darker shade to accent trim and railings, and a water-like blue-gray on the deck.

FLUID LINES

This striking multilevel deck design (left) integrates fully with the house in style, color, and composition. Open, fluid railings allow spa users to keep others in view and experience the beauty of the natural scenery. Plexiglass inserts keep children safe without blocking views. Design: Peter C. Kurth Office of Architecture and Planning.

WINDOWS BRING THE OUTDOORS IN

One of the elements that sets contemporary architecture apart from many traditional styles is its emphasis on large expanses of glass to visually connect the inside with the outside world and to bring an abundance of natural light to interior spaces. When grouped closely together with rhythmic regularity, large windows and glass doors give a house a sense of transparency, breaking down the barriers usually set up by walls.

This openness contributes to the success of many deck designs found in contemporary settings and allows dramatic indoor-outdoor relationships that are not possible with more traditional homes. The deck becomes a true extension of the interior—a continuation of the floor plan—and the rooms inside take on a new dimension when viewed from the deck. This open arrangement also permits more flexibility when activities occur, whether it's parents watching children at play or the hostess in the kitchen keeping an eye on guests and the barbecue outside.

DOUBLE VISION

Following the contours of this window-lined home, an expansive and well-furnished deck (left) enjoys views of indoor spaces as well as the outdoor surroundings. The restful neutral color scheme of the house and deck is punctuated with vivid red accents for visual interest.

WINDOW EXPANSION

A multitude of windows along the rear facade of this contemporary home (right) opens it up to light and broad vistas. Painted to blend with the exterior, the deck railing and stairs have a substantial feel that suits the building's size. An open framework at ground level maintains views from the lowest floor. Design: R. J. Kietzman. Windows: Norco Windows, Inc.

DESIGNED TO CAPTURE VIEWS

A site that's open to a panoramic view provides wonderful opportunities for orienting and styling a house and its deck to take advantage of the magnificent vistas. The clean architectural lines and large expanses of glass that characterize many contemporary homes permit virtually unimpeded views from interior living areas, and when there's room for a deck, the pleasure extends well into the outdoors.

Because decks have flexibility in placement, shape, and size, they can easily be custom-crafted to fit where they function best. When unobstructed views are a priority, one solution is to design a series of levels spreading down and away from the house. This arrangement allows those seated indoors and on the upper levels to look across and beyond the areas below, usually without the visual interference of furnishings or railings. When a site permits an on-grade or slightly raised deck, another solution might be to construct a broad platform that uses low benches and planters to provide safety while maximizing both close-in and distant views.

OUTDOOR PLEASURE

Expansive views from indoors and out prompted a low-profile deck design for this cedar-clad contemporary home (right). The changing patterns of the deck's cedar floorboards and the judicious placement of railing, steps, and planters help delineate the level changes. Home and deck design: Lindal Cedar Homes.

OPEN VIEW

Perched high above the rest of the world, this small yet dramatic deck (left) captures a spectacular panorama. The steep site dictated a series of small interconnected levels cascading downhill. Home and deck design: Lindal Cedar Homes.

TRANSFORMING A BORING BACKYARD

As the suburban population grows and houses adjust to smaller lots and other restrictions, decks are coming into their own as functional, pleasing alternatives to the traditional backyard. Unlike lawns and most patios, decks can run right up to the door at the same level as the interior rooms, becoming true extensions of the home. They can follow the lay of the land or strike out on an individual course that creates its own landscape. Decks can also be fashioned and finished in exactly the same materials, colors, and textures as the houses they adjoin, bringing cohesiveness to the entire indoor-outdoor area.

The two-tiered redwood deck pictured here was designed as a friendly takeover of an uninteresting yet high maintenance backyard that sat well below the house and had little connection with the indoor living areas. Stretching the width of the lot, the new deck includes amenities the former space could only dream of: an aboveground swimming pool, conversation and dining areas, built-in planters requiring little upkeep, and a trellis to provide afternoon shade and privacy from neighbors.

A BETTER BACKYARD

A perfect complement to the house in style, color, and material, this multilevel redwood deck (left) offers all the pleasures of outdoor living without the hassles of backyard maintenance. Although the deck system is raised well above the ground, clever planning makes it appear to follow the lay of the land.

SIMPLE LOOKS AND A SNUG FIT

Decks often get the most use when they edge the living areas and are easily reached from several rooms. Following the house perimeter, wrapping around corners, and tucking into nooks, they also serve as handy outdoor routes to various parts of the home. Much of contemporary American architecture, with its emphasis on informality and uncluttered lines, lends itself to these practical, uncomplicated deck designs. They can work especially well with single-story designs, helping to enlarge and dress up a modest rectangular shape, for instance, or unify a plan that has a series of ells or projecting wings.

Simple materials suit these versatile wraparound decks. Vertical wood siding pairs nicely with the horizontal lines of decking, and when both surfaces have weathered to a soft gray, they gain extra appeal. The smooth appearance of vertical siding also makes it a good backdrop for simply styled railings, stairs, and benches.

PRIVATE AREA

The clean, uncluttered lines of this contemporary house (above) are in perfect harmony with its snugly fitted deck. The neutral palette of all wood surfaces also adds to the harmony. Enclosed by the house, the deck serves as a completely private outdoor room and a connector to indoor living spaces.

TWO STYLES

A metal roof and skylights give a contemporary look to this ranch house (left) while its wraparound deck is dressed in country attire. Green park benches provide places to sit in the sun or shade. Design and construction: Yankee Barn Homes.

GRACEFUL EXPANSION

Edging the perimeter of an expansive brick and wood home, this deck (above) gradually spills down to a built-in seating area. The white metal railing adds contrast to the wood deck. Design: The Brickman Group.

REMODELED IN A COMPELLING STYLE

Many houses constructed in the last 25 years included a deck in the original building plan. While it was usually functional, it was ordinary in appearance. The typical deck consisted of a plain rectangular platform edged with a crib-style railing that usually projected off the rear facade and only sometimes included stairs to the ground. If that sounds too familiar, sometimes a remodel is just what a deck needs to lift it from mundane to extraordinary.

The dramatic deck seen here fit this plain-Jane description before its remodel. It had no access to the backyard at all, and, worse, it detracted from the striking contemporary architecture of the house. The deck's dynamic redesign echoes the precise lines and clean crisp styling of the building and connects the deck to the lawn. Following the sloping site, the three levels make the transition from the living areas to the yard a pleasant experience, with built-in benches and planters to accompany the route. Clear plexiglass inserts in the railing provide safety and allow unobstructed views of the surrounding landscape.

NEW AND IMPROVED

The contemporary styling of the house (right) set the theme for this multilevel replacement deck, which descends 20 feet to the lawn. The roughly sawn cedar siding of the deck walls matches the house in material and color. Design: Peter C. Kurth Office of Architecture and Planning.

UP-TO-DATE PLANS

The original 1970s-built deck was updated and enlarged into a series of levels and stairs that gradually lead to the ground (left). The floorboards change direction on the midlevel landing to draw attention to the steps and provide visual interest. Deck plans: Peter C. Kurth Office of Architecture and Planning.

HI-TECH TOUCHES ADD ZEST AND COLOR

A deck doesn't have to be limited to an all-wood design to complement a wood-clad house. Changing the material of the railing is one of the easiest ways to vary a deck's look and mood. A tubular rail, for instance, can inject a hi-tech note and lend a more contemporary feeling to the overall design.

The 50s-era home shown here got a zesty facelift with a redwood replacement deck highlighted by a railing made of steel-tubing and finished in an exuberant red. To give the fairly narrow deck a little more elbow room, two triangular popouts were added along with built-in seating, eliminating the need for bulky furniture. New French doors replace aluminum windows and permit access from three major areas of the house—the living room, dining room, and kitchen. A series of stairs and landings segregates various activities, such as dining or relaxing in the hot tub, and provides an easy route to the backyard. The painted redwood siding of the lower portion of the deck blends in with the existing house while its diagonal pattern updates the building's appearance.

HI-TECH ACCENTS

Glossy red railings (above) add zest while complementing the rich tones of the redwood stairs and landings. The midlevel spa is accessible from the house yet remains hidden from those dining or relaxing on the main deck.
Design: Garry Papers Architecture & Design.

EXTRA FEATURES

Deck posts and substructure are enclosed in diagonal wood siding that harmonizes with the existing horizontal boards of the house (right). The frames above the French doors will soon be entwined with wisteria to shade this south-facing wall year round.
Design: Garry Papers Architecture & Design.

STYLISH REVISION

Sleek steel tubing edges this deck (above), giving it a contemporary look and drawing the eye to the triangular sitting areas. The redwood floorboards were screwed in place from underneath for a smooth, fastener-free finish. Design: Garry Papers Architecture & Design.

SPACIOUS PLATFORMS TO THE YARD

A large lot with a spacious home invites an equally spacious deck that matches the size and proportions of the house as well as its style. A big two-story structure like this one would overwhelm a pint-size deck, making it seem lost in the overall design. From a purely practical point of view, a large house will be far more livable and functional if its outdoor living areas are equally roomy, providing enough space for a number of different activities.

When a site is fairly level and there's plenty of open space, a large deck can spread out into the landscape on broad platforms or levels, easing the transition from house to yard and turning the journey into a leisurely stroll. Large decks are also suited to widely spaced furniture groupings in well-separated activity areas, which can be welcome if several age groups—toddlers, teens, and grandparents—are using the deck at the same time.

CLASSIC PROPORTION

The distinctive architecture and rambling layout of this home (left) called for a spacious deck that would not compete visually with the design. The nearly level site allows the deck to spread gradually into the yard. A number of places to sit and dine makes for a versatile living area. Design and construction: Yankee Barn Homes.

TIGHT SPACES PUT TO GOOD USE

Whether due to the nature of the site or simply because outdoor space is at a premium, there may be limited space for a deck. A spatial challenge like that requires creative solutions. One approach that can work well with hard-to-reach or confined outdoor areas is a modular deck system. A modular deck is composed of sections prebuilt at a shop (or in the garage) and then assembled on-site. Often only the floor decking itself is the modular component, but stairs, seating, and railings may also be prefabricated into sections that are handy to transport and quick to assemble. This versatile approach can also save on construction labor and expense.

Another solution to the small-space dilemma is tailoring the deck to an "exact fit," making use of every available inch. That might mean sandwiching a simple platform deck between a fence and the house or shaping a more complex design into a series of tightly interconnected levels. Revamping a small lackluster area might also be the answer. For instance, converting narrow back steps and a concrete walkway into a few broad landings with built-in benches and planters would still provide access to and from the house while encouraging outdoor living.

CREATIVE SOLUTION

A modular deck system came to the rescue when a steep downslope prevented conventional solutions. One of three similar redwood decks, all connected by stairs, this ground-level unit (right) is comprised of six-foot hexagonal sections arranged in a concentric pattern. Modular railings, bench, and planters follow the hexagonal theme. The spiral stairs are steel sections dressed up with a redwood decking inlay.

TAILORED TO FIT

An uninspiring portion of a yard got a fresh start with a handsome cedar deck (left) that's small in size but big on looks. The ground-hugging deck fits snugly between the existing concrete walkway and a wall of trees. A well-thought-out stair design shields the deck area from the street and offers landings roomy enough for a chair or two. Cedar lattice screening keeps understair storage conveniently out of sight. Design and construction: Dennis Elliot. Deck furniture and accessories: Sun Gallery and Dig This.

DECK RETREAT IN THE MOUNTAINS

Graceful and unobtrusive, the built-in redwood benches edging the deck (below) were designed to allow filtered views while providing comfortable, ergonomically correct seating. The little corner table adds a light yet practical touch. Design and construction: Scott Padgett.

Vacation retreats in the mountains are often tucked into rustic settings that are ideally suited to decks. An abundance of trees, nearby wildlife, brisk starry nights, and an informal approach to living are all part of the outdoor experience that can be enjoyed from a deck.

This redwood home enjoyed a mountain atmosphere but, originally built without a deck, lacked a functional outdoor area for the owners to enjoy the sights and sounds of a seasonal creek and small waterfalls that lay a short distance from the house. The site, though picturesque, was rocky, steep, and confined. The solution was a bi-level redwood deck that sits low to the ground and steps down a gentle portion of the grade to a landing near the creek. The connecting stairs, angled to fit between existing rocks and along a stone wall, seem to float as they gradually narrow and descend to the ground. Built-in benches and an integrated railing were designed in a light, open style so they would not block outside views from the interior rooms.

A new redwood deck (right) matches the style, color, and mood of this rustic mountain retreat to harmoniously blend in with the wooded setting. Designed to fit into the existing landscape rather than alter it, the deck's levels and steps angle around rocks and trees on their gentle descent to a nearby creek. Design and construction: Scott Padgett.

MULTIPLE ACCESS POINTS

For maximum enjoyment and pure practicality, nothing can beat a deck that features several places to move back and forth from the outdoors to the interior. Having multiple access points also gives a deck flexibility in the way it functions and underscores its role as an extension of the house and its living spaces. A deck that's accessible from a number of areas can lessen some of the wear and tear caused by foot traffic that would normally travel down the hallway, for instance, and cut across the family room to get outside.

When two or three rooms open onto a deck, the overall space can be divided into informal zones that host different functions. Comfortable furnishings might be grouped near the living room; the barbecue can be positioned off the kitchen and not far from the dining table and chairs. And when a deck design incorporates more than one level, each accessed from a different point, the outdoor area can be home to individual "rooms" geared to specific activities.

EASY ACCESS

Whether reaching the deck from the house or the yard, this thoughtful design (right) offers a number of places to come and go. As it wraps around the new screened-in porch, the deck uses built-in benches, planters, and a meandering rail to divide the large area into outdoor "rooms." Pressure-treated lumber: Wolmanized Lumber.

ACCESS FOR LENGTHY DECKS

All decks function better with several entrances, but designs that stretch across a long facade on a single level are especially good candidates for multiple places to move indoors and out. Without adequate access, parts of the deck can become a wasted space that is seldom used since it's difficult to reach or inconveniently far from the rooms it was meant to serve.

In general, a lengthy deck should incorporate a minimum of three access points from different living areas. Door openings should be wide enough for two people to pass through comfortably at the same time; French doors, atrium-style folding doors, and sliding glass doors work best for this task. A series of double doors along the house facade can also help give the deck continuity and keep the overall design in better balance.

Rambling decks are more interesting when the expanse is broken up visually and details are given extra attention. A slight change in level, the presence of stairs, built-in benches, shade overhangs, and even an unusual railing treatment or a change in direction of floorboards can relieve monotony and transform the area into a welcoming outdoor room.

RAMBLING DECK

Multiple French doors ease movement to and from the house (left) and also take in views of the surrounding woods. The railing design echoes the horizontal lines of the house while the deck's angular shape offsets the flat facade. Design and construction: Yankee Barn Homes.

INVITING DESIGN

The handsome posts and traditional-style railing bordering this rather long, narrow deck (below) give the area definition and harmonize with the brickwork and house trim. The deck floor is divided into sections to help break up its length visually and to indicate access points.

COLOR ENLIVENS A NEW VICTORIAN

American houses of the Victorian period, spanning roughly the second half of the 19th century, varied from high-style mansions embellished with turrets, huge wraparound porches, and fancy gingerbread trim to typical family dwellings found across the country that incorporated Victorian finery in more modest ways. One common theme shared by many Victorian designs was the use of color to differentiate parts of the house or to highlight a special element, such as lacy fretwork or an intricately carved door. House painters of the era would use as many as ten different colors. And although pastels were popular, some houses wore deeper, more intense shades while others displayed brilliant hues.

The updated version of a 19th-century Victorian shown here carries some of the features associated with the styles of the time, including the use of color to draw attention to exterior detailing. The presence of a roomy deck off the rear porch, however, is a thoroughly modern addition, extending the living areas out into the open, easing the transition from the house down to the backyard, and providing a spacious outdoor room for all kinds of activities.

CLASSIC DETAILS

Victorian styling characterizes this picturesque rear porch (right), from the spindles and fretwork near the ceiling to the turned posts of the railing to the painted floor. A level below the shady porch, a roomy deck provides places to sit in the sun and enjoy wide-open views. Design: Home Planners, Inc.

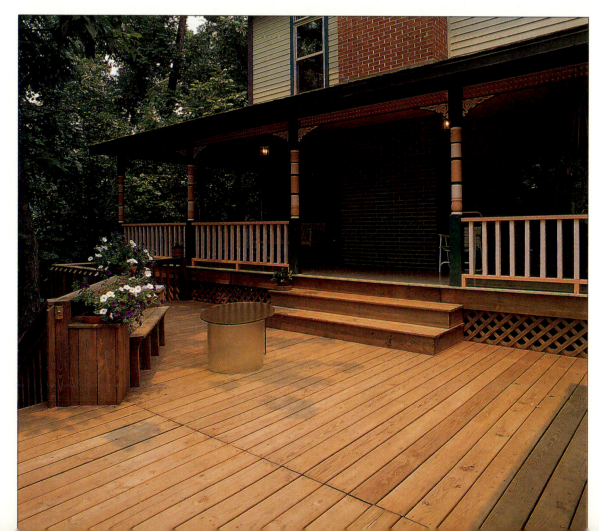

A MODERN ADDITION

The natural wood tones of the deck (right) blend nicely with the light tint of the house facade; together they create a neutral backdrop for the lively colors that accentuate the gutters, trim, and porch detailing. Design: Home Planners, Inc.

UNPRETENTIOUS DECK DESIGNS

Traditional styles aren't always tied to a certain period of the past or a type of formal architecture. Sometimes a traditional-feeling home is simply a warm, informal, rustic design reminiscent of a barn, perhaps, or a farmhouse, cottage, or bungalow. The decks and porches of these agreeable homes are usually equally inviting, serving as comfortable outdoor living areas that welcome users like an old friend. These cozy decks are often modest in size, simply constructed, and unpretentious in appearance. As such, they can allow the traditional features of the house to stand out more prominently. They can also serve as perfect backdrops for a colorful garden or an attractively landscaped yard.

SIMPLE PLEASURE

Rustic barn siding, divided-lite windows, and a dormered roof give traditional flavor to this informal home (right). Its simple, shady deck complements the house and setting comfortably. The stone table and terra cotta flowerpot lend the deck area a bit of interest.

GARDEN SETTING

An inviting little deck (left) nestles close to the back door of an older brick home. Potted plants and a profusion of vibrant flowers enliven its weathered surfaces and dress up the gray and white color scheme of the house. The birdhouse on top of the shade structure adds a whimsical touch.

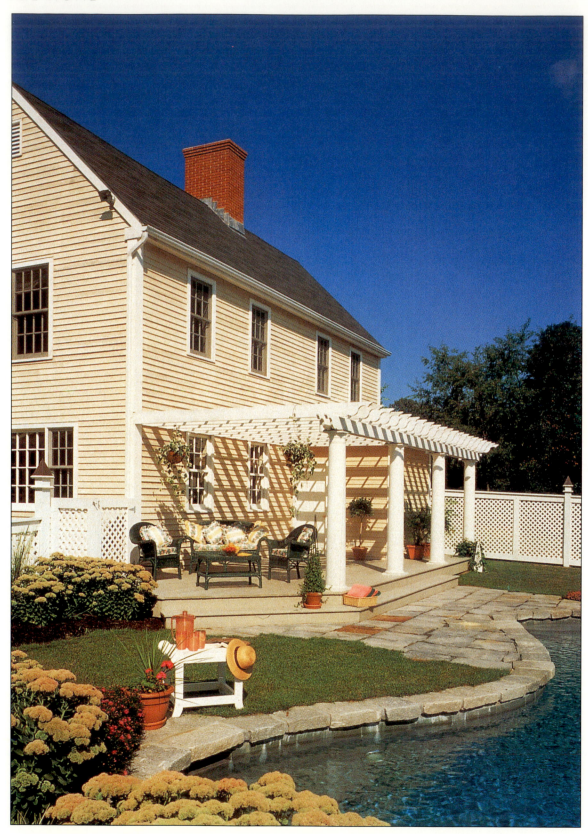

TOUCH OF CLASS

A traditional New England Colonial (right) adopts a classical air with a colonnaded deck overlooking the pool. The well-proportioned columns have a solid appearance that contrasts nicely with the open framework of the pergola and the latticework of the surrounding fence. Design: Dan Haslegrave.

CLASSICAL REFERENCES

Architectural styles adapted from the classic orders of Greek and Roman design have appeared in American buildings since the 1700s. Early Southern Colonial mansions were graced with colonnades that provided shade yet were open to light and breezes. Georgian designs included grand entrances with a pedimented roof supported by columns. Roman "villas," such as Thomas Jefferson's Monticello, incorporated outdoor walkways and pergolas. The Greek revival style became so popular in the mid-1800s that carpenters brought it to the new homes of America.

Architects today continue to integrate classical principles into their designs—some boldly, others with just a reference. Decks can take especially well to the classics, too, whether it's maintaining the correct proportions for the size and scale of the house, bringing balance or symmetry to the shape of the floor, or adding detail to the overhead shelter.

A MODERN CLASSIC

Balance, symmetry, and a bold design characterize this neoclassic deck and spa surround (left). Modern materials such as the fiberglass spa and prefabricated columns give a new dimension to the classical theme. A spiral staircase connects a second-story bedroom to a private, screened redwood deck. Spa: Caldera Spas & Bath.

TRADITIONAL LOOKS WITHOUT WOOD

Traditional detailing gives this small rear deck (below) an old-fashioned flavor. Floor boards, railings, and a latticework skirt have the appearance of painted wood, but they are fabricated from PVC vinyl and will never need repainting. PVC decking: Heritage Vinyl Products.

Although wood has traditionally been associated with decks, it is a material that requires maintenance to keep it healthy and looking its best. In wet environments, wood can be subject to decay; where it's hot, wood can crack and splinter from exposure to the sun's ultra-violet rays. A deck that's not properly sealed can be host to mildew. Painted surfaces need extra upkeep. And the natural color of nearly any wood deck will fade in time.

One practical alternative to the drawbacks of wood is a synthetic decking material such as a PVC vinyl. Formulated to be weather-resistant and virtually maintenance-free, PVC vinyl decks are durable, do not crack or warp, and never need painting. This type of decking is available with traditional or contemporary looks and offers a number of railing designs that can harmonize with a variety of house styles.

Pleasantly situated amid grassy backyards, this PVC vinyl deck (right) makes a charming little gathering place for entertaining neighbors. Sturdily built, splinter-free, and a breeze to keep clean, the deck is also a great spot for children to play. PVC decking: Brock Manufacturing.

CRAFTSMAN THEMES FIND A HOME

The Craftsman style of architecture emerged in the early 1900s. It was a movement dedicated to bringing simplicity, beauty, and "honesty" to home-building through traditional craftsmanship and materials. It had its strongest following in the American West and produced both large and small houses of diverse design, including the familiar bungalow. This style sought to use wood expressively, exposing timbers and shaping and fitting them together in bold yet rhythmic lines. Many Craftsman designs also took a comprehensive approach to the house and its surroundings, incorporating gardens and outdoor living areas as planned extensions of the home—a common theme now but not widely practiced in other styles of the era.

In addition, a keen interest in Japanese art and workmanship among artisans and architects brought a Japanese flavor to many of these designs. Drawing on principles honored by American and Japanese artisans, the style synthesized into a comfortable hybrid that characterizes a number of homes built in more recent years.

INFLUENCED STYLE

Exposed beams and rafters, projecting eaves, and a simple but expressive use of wood shows the Craftsman influence in both the house and deck design (right). The furnishings, too, express a Craftsman theme, modeled after the mission style. Design: Ken Dahlin. CCA-treated hem-fir deck: McFarland Cascade.

NATURAL HYBRID

A Japanese feeling characterizes the deck and its pergola-style seating area (right). An emphasis on horizontal lines and a direct, if restrained, use of wood give the area a serenity that fits the secluded setting. The angled rafter ends of the overhead shelter are typical of the Craftsman touch. Design: Ken Dahlin. CCA-treated hem-fir deck: McFarland Cascade.

A NEW DECK HIDES AN OLD PATIO

Built in the 1930s as a Craftsman-style cabin meant for weekend and vacation getaways, this shingled mountain home grew sequentially over the years into a larger, permanent residence. The original concrete patio, however, remained untouched until recently when a handsome redwood deck was devised to cover the unsightly slab and give the home an attractive, accessible outdoor space on the same level as the interior rooms.

Wrapping around the front and side of the house, the semicircular deck provides a visual continuity that makes the area seem much larger than its 550 square feet. The rustic simplicity of the redwood floor, scattered with occasional knots and streaked sapwood, serves as a subdued background for the graceful railing that follows the curved edge. Inspired by themes found in Craftsman-style architecture and Japanese art, the finely detailed railing and the handmade redwood and copper lights provide the finishing touches to this charming vintage home.

REFINED CHARM

The handsome redwood deck (left) edging this mountain home covers a 1930s patio that had deteriorated with age. The wraparound deck features a finely crafted railing and custom light fixtures that pay homage to the Craftsman style. Design and construction: Scott Padgett.

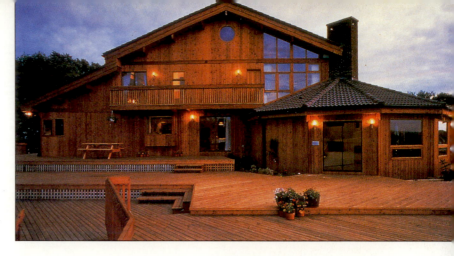

REGIONAL INFLUENCES AND MATERIALS

The "regional" house relates to its setting more intimately than most, fitting not only the site but adapting to local geography and climate by using materials that are native to the region and often embracing styles that historically "belong." American regional, or vernacular, architecture evolved over the years as a sensible response to climate and site that also took advantage of whatever materials were readily available. The wood clapboard houses of New England had small windows and large fireplaces to help minimize the cold; adobe designs of the Southwest employed extra-thick walls to keep out the heat.

The regional styles of the Pacific Northwest reflect a composite of shapes, materials, and moods, which are influenced by its diverse history and culture. Although the styles of the houses shown here are somewhat different, they respond to local conditions in similar ways. Ample decks suggest comfortable temperatures and sunny skies for most of the year while large expanses of glass offset overcast periods by bringing light and views to the interiors. All feature local western red cedar siding and decks finished to allow the wood's natural beauty to shine through.

OUTDOOR ENJOYMENT

Typical of Northwestern styles, a Japanese influence is seen in this home's tiled roof, uncluttered lines, and respect for wood in its natural form (above). The restrained, sparse design of the broad platform deck suggests an area meant for transitions from interior spaces to the landscape. Home and deck design: Lindal Cedar Homes.

ALPINE RETREAT

A familiar sight amid the mountains of the West, this A-frame (right) easily adapts to alpine conditions. Informal living areas open to a well-proportioned deck that wraps around a sky-lit wing. Home and deck design: Lindal Cedar Homes.

YEAR-ROUND APPEAL

The glass-enclosed sunroom between house and deck (right) is a perfect solution for year-round living, especially in regions where it's often too cool or damp during the summer to enjoy the deck on a regular basis. In winter, it can collect the sun's warmth and distribute it to interior rooms. Home and deck design: Lindal Cedar Homes.

IN THE JAPANESE TRADITION

For centuries, the Japanese have created gardens for the quiet contemplation of natural beauty. These tranquil places nearly always incorporate stone into their design and show restraint in the use of plants. A traditional Japanese-style garden might use sand or stone chips to form a "sea" spreading across the ground, interrupted by small islands of rocks, pavers, and low shrubs. A water feature might also be present—perhaps a little pool, pond, or stream.

This serene deck design with an artful blend of redwood and stone draws inspiration from the Japanese concept of harmony with nature. Terraced into three levels, the redwood deck spreads like a sea around a stone-edged pool and spa, the surrounding panorama interrupted only slightly by an occasional planter or shrub and a light-feeling rail.

The former deck and existing pool and spa were ill-fitted to the site and to each other. This dramatic solution integrates these elements into a sweeping yet functional design that relates to the landscape and takes in the views. On the main level, stone pavers sit flush with the deck floor, serving to ease visual transitions between pool, deck, and spa. Tucked close to the house and sheltered by the broad branches of a pine tree, the area around the spa is a more intimate space but still open to the surrounding vista.

IN HARMONY WITH NATURE

Inspired by Japanese design principles, this spacious deck and pool area (right) is the crowning touch to a dramatic if difficult site. Built on three levels so as to step down with the land without impeding the views, the redwood deck surrounds an existing pool and a spa now edged with natural stone. The beautifully integrated design demonstrates the simplicity, restraint, and harmony found in Japanese gardens. Design: David Reed.

AN OLDER TUDOR GAINS A NEW DECK

In the early 20th century, a number of traditional architectural styles were revived all around the country. Many of these designs were rooted in certain periods of history, both American and European. One of the more popular period styles was the Tudor, usually a simplified version of the Elizabethan house and distinguished by its stuccoed or stone exterior, exposed half-timbers, and small leaded windows.

The redwood deck addition shown here blends handsomely with the picturesque style of the Tudor home. The gabled structure above the French doors echoes the shape of the roof lines, its timber-frame construction also a reminder of the Tudor's characteristic half-timbers. Neatly wrapped with redwood siding, the well-integrated deck design visually anchors the house to the ground and gives presence to a sideyard that was ignored before. Dark-stained surfaces tie in with the house trim and the shingled upper walls and give the deck a more traditional look.

CUSTOM DETAILS

The timber-framed overhead structure (above) mimics the roof shape, defines the stairway from the yard to the door, and helps visually tie the house and deck together. The dark finish on the new wood surfaces mirrors the color of the house trim. Design and construction: Joseph D. Wood.

SPECIAL FEATURES

Artistically wrapped with a redwood surround, the built-in spa (left) features a curving bench that also serves as a step for easing in and out of the water. Trees and hedging provide a natural privacy screen for bathers. Design and construction: Joseph D. Wood.

BLENDED STYLE

The beautifully crafted elements of this redwood deck (right) complement the traditional styling of this Tudor home. The balusters of the railing carry a whimsical heart motif. Other custom touches can be seen in the carved handrail and mahogany ventilation grates along the deck skirt. Design and construction: Joseph D. Wood.

NATURALISTIC SETTING FOR A DECK

A thoughtful landscape design can do wonders to unify a house and its outdoor living areas. And taking a naturalistic approach is an especially pleasing way to tie the various elements together. Simply stated, "naturalistic" designs seek to recreate a little piece of nature that might have been there all along. They usually integrate stone—boulders, river rocks, pavers, and even pebbles—with permanent plantings such as low shrubs, ground covers, and small trees. Ideally, the design offers different textures, heights, and colors—several shades of green, for instance—and may even incorporate fragrance into the plan. This style of landscape is helpful in softening the sometimes "hard" look of a newly built deck.

In the landscape design shown here, the naturalistic swimming pool—more a pond than a pool in mood and appearance—is the key element that ties the simply styled house and its deck to a number of outdoor living areas. As the deck cascades down to a brick patio edging the pool, it seems to flow into the landscape, spilling around the pool on its way to the wood-rimmed spa and screened sitting area.

NATURAL STYLE

A cedar deck (right) descends to a naturalistic pool in a series of platforms to join with a patio that stretches into the garden setting. The cedar-ringed spa at one edge of the patio is intended to resemble a dock on the bank of a little pond. A small waterfall and plantings inspired by Oriental gardens round out the pool design. Design: Stuart Narofsky.

AMENITIES FOR THE DECK

While a deck design can often function perfectly well on its own, there are times when a special feature can add to its comfort or convenience and make it more attractive as well. A deck that's completely exposed to the sun, for instance, will be used and enjoyed throughout more of the day if it has some sort of shade, whether provided by an overhead shelter or the canopy of a tree. Outdoor cooking will proceed more smoothly if there's a handy place near the barbecue to set down dishes and store utensils. A spa outside the bedroom will be all the more relaxing with the presence of a privacy screen to shield the area from neighbors or the street.

While some amenities are intended to satisfy particular needs and are geared primarily to activities on the deck, others can improve the overall design of the yard. A thoughtful deck extension can provide better access to the swimming pool and incorporate places to sit in sun or shade. A garden structure, such as a gazebo or an arbor, set at a distance from the main deck can create a retreat that seems miles away.

This chapter shows some of the special services decks can perform and highlights a few of the features that can make them more useful.

FENCED-IN PRIVACY

The redwood fence bordering this serene deck and pool design (right) provides privacy from neighboring houses while the louvered boards allow glimpses of the landscape. The new redwood platform deck floats above an existing pool.

OUTDOOR LIVING ON THE PORCH

As American as apple pie, the traditional porch holds a special place in most hearts, whether it faces the street, wraps around to the side, or overlooks the backyard. Porches evoke memories of a less hurried way of life—sitting on the swing to watch the moon rise, and children selling lemonade at the foot of the steps to thirsty passersby.

Under cover but open to air, light, and the surrounding scene, porches can bridge the space between the outdoors and the house interior in a number of ways. A small front porch or stoop shelters the door but doesn't invite a long stay, whereas a long porch spanning the width of the house encourages visitors to linger at the rail or rest in wicker chairs. Porches can make a modest cottage seem larger and give a rather ordinary design a grander appearance. Furnished and accented with plants, they can turn into outdoor living and dining rooms. Most of all, porches increase a home's livability in a warm, informal way.

ALL-AMERICAN

Brimming with Victorian charm, this balconied front porch (left) represents a traditional American design found in small towns across the country just a century ago. What better place to spend a warm afternoon sipping iced tea, chatting with friends, and waving to neighbors walking by.

AREA EXTENSION

French doors opening on two sides to this simply styled wraparound porch, or veranda (right), extend indoor spaces outward. The stylish doors help transform the veranda into a gracious outdoor living room. Design and construction: Yankee Barn Homes.

QUIET CHARM

An old-fashioned feeling pervades this porch (below). The wedge pattern of the floorboards follows the angular path of the posts and railings, adding interest to the overall design. Pressure-treated lumber: Wolmanized Lumber.

OLD-STYLE PORCHES FOR NEW HOMES

Porches are typically associated with older homes and bygone eras, but many current house designs integrate front and rear porches into the original plan as a way to expand living space without adding another interior room. With more and more families following informal lifestyles and discovering the pleasures of relaxing and entertaining at home, porches are joining decks and patios as multifunctional indoor-outdoor areas. And although porches most often accompany traditional designs—shingled Victorians, Midwestern farmhouses, rambling ranches—they have also found a place among more contemporary styles. Because porches are constructed as an integral part of a house, often sharing the same foundation and roof system, they adapt to the same site conditions. They may sit on-grade with the floor just slightly above the ground, or they may be raised a distance off the ground and connected to the yard with stairs. Like most attached decks, the porch floor nearly always lies on or very near the same level as interior rooms, easing the transition between indoors and out. Unlike many decks, however, a porch usually remains on a single continuous level as it edges the house.

UPDATED STYLE

In this modern rendition of the traditional front porch, a broad entry deck (right) serves as a transitional area between front lawn and house. Wood benches painted a crisp white to match the porch detailing help integrate the two spaces. Design: Todd Soli Architects.

BRINGING PRIVACY TO A DECK

A privacy screen is often an essential ingredient in a deck plan, especially when neighboring houses sit too close for comfort or have direct views of the deck. Screens can be fencelike in appearance, for ultimate privacy, or more open in design to allow light and air to filter through. When paired with an overhead covering, they can create the impression of an outdoor room. The open construction of a simple trellis offers a measure of privacy; when backed by shrubbery or covered with vines, however, it can be as effective as a solid fence.

Vertical screens are helpful additions where conditions are windy or the sun's angle overheats the deck from the side. Around a pool or spa, they can prevent leaves and debris from blowing into the water and cut the wind's chill, making the deck area a more pleasant place to use and easier to maintain.

OUTDOOR RETREAT

A porchlike setting and the use of comfortable wicker furnishings transform this deck (above) into an outdoor room with a nostalgic feel. Tightly woven lattice atop the railing affords privacy and filtered sunlight. Design: Dalla Lana Griffin.

SECLUDED GARDEN

A private hideaway in the midst of town, this deck (right) and its components work together in harmony with the shape and scale of the house. The sunken rock garden supplies a change of texture and color. Design: Dennis' Seven Dees Landscaping. ACQ-treated Douglas fir deck: J.H. Baxter & Company.

QUIET DETAIL

The intricate geometric cutout in this redwood privacy screen (left) creates an unusual design and provides selected views from a nearby spa. Open detailing at the top softens the fence below and ties in aesthetically with the structure overhead. Design and construction: Timothy R. Bitts, Sun Wave Construction.

SCREENED COMFORT, RAIN OR SHINE

Nothing can dampen spirits more than a rained-out barbecue—unless it's fighting off pesky insects that arrive rain or shine. A screened enclosure can take the edge off the less desirable aspects of outdoor living while still providing pleasurable breezes, sights, and sounds. It makes an ideal playroom for housebound kids on a rainy day and a welcome place to camp out on hot summer nights.

Screened-in porches were common features on homes built earlier this century, especially in warmer regions of the country. Once the deck and patio replaced the lawn as the primary outdoor living space, though, the screened porch often gave way to an additional interior room. An existing porch can be easily screened in; if it sits at the side or rear of the house or near the kitchen, it can serve as a truly private outdoor room for dining or entertaining. Enclosing a portion of a deck that lies close to the house is another option and a way to enjoy the safety of screening just steps away from the great outdoors.

OUTDOOR SERENITY

This porch addition (above) offers all the comforts of home in screened protection from bothersome insects and inclement weather. Positioned at the back of the house, the porch has privacy, too, and opens to a small deck at one side. Pressure-treated lumber: Wolmanized Lumber.

DOUBLE-DUTY

This arrangement (right) combines the best of both worlds: escape from the heat in a shady screened room and sunshine out on the deck. The low-level deck also serves as a transition between the yard and the house. Pressure-treated lumber: Wolmanized Lumber.

SCENIC HIDEAWAY

What better retreat for reading or relaxing on a rainy day than a screened porch with a view (above), especially when flowering shrubs and trees are at their prime and greenery lies all around.

SURROUNDS FOR SPA SOAKING

Whether you think of a soak in a spa as therapeutic or just plain fun, integrating a spa into a deck design can be accomplished with relative ease. Unlike swimming pools, spas take up little room and can be incorporated into small-space decks tucked into a tight corner or a narrow sideyard. They are most enjoyed when located in a quiet spot not too far from the house, shielded from wind and neighbors.

Although the typical spa lies nearly flush with its surround, it can be designed to rise above the floor, hot-tub style. Despite appearances, spas and hot tubs are seldom supported by the decking itself; they usually rest directly on the ground or on a portion of the deck substructure. Since they are not structural, deck surrounds can be laid out in countless ways to create dramatic floor patterns, accentuate the soaking area, or simply echo the shape of the spa.

EASY ACCESS

The central attraction of this multilevel deck (above), an octagonal spa is easy to reach from upper and lower platforms. Freestanding benches can be pulled close to the spa's edge so people can dangle their feet in the water. Lumber: Georgia Pacific Corp.

ULTIMATE SPA

This soaring redwood pavilion (left) commands attention to its sturdy timber-frame construction and its role as a beautiful yet functional shade structure. Part of an expansive redwood deck situated amid the trees, the area surrounding the 8 × 12-foot spa features several places to sit. Design and construction: Bryan Hays.

OUTDOOR ENJOYMENT

Simple yet stunning, this cedar spa surround (right) tucks snugly between a new master bedroom and a beautiful landscape. Because the site dictated an on-grade deck, the spa rises above the floor. A cedar skirt dresses up its sides and unifies the design. Design: Showplace Kitchens & Baths.

SURROUNDS FOR SWIMMING

Refreshing, invigorating, and fun for all ages, swimming pools add hours of pleasure to outdoor living. Because pools are often the dominant element in the yard, the manner in which they're surrounded can make a difference between just adequate and simply terrific.

Because of its versatility, wood decking makes an excellent choice for all or part of a pool surround. Wood integrates well with other materials often found around a pool—tile, brick, natural stone—and decking can be designed to adopt nearly any shape the area requires. If the ground around the pool is uneven or sloped, wood decking is sometimes the best solution.

Generally speaking, the surround should be at least equal in size to the area of the pool (preferably larger) to allow enough room for a table, chairs, and a variety of seating options. A shady place nearby to seek relief from the sun is desirable as well. A surround that covers a large expanse seems friendlier when broken into levels and treated as several outdoor rooms. Changing the direction and pattern of the boards can help scale down a large deck, too. By contrast, a surround that has to fit a tight spot seems larger if edged with built-in benches that take up little space but provide places to sit or stretch out in the sun.

A NEW DIRECTION

An existing pool (below) takes on a new dimension with a refreshing redwood surround that wraps around the water with diagonal deck boards. Projecting into the sloping yard a step up from the rest of the deck, a sheltered sitting area carries its boards in the opposite direction to visually separate it. Design and construction: Jamie Turrentine.

NATURAL HARMONY

The rich colors and textures of the redwood and brick deck surrounding this 35-foot lap pool (left) blend harmoniously with the natural landscape. The gently curved design is an eye-pleasing, dramatic solution to gaining outdoor living space on a steep and rocky site that previously had no use. The trellis at the end of the pool screens the area from a nearby street. Design: Scott E. Smith.

OUTDOOR COOKING AT ITS BEST

Nothing beats cooking outdoors on a warm summer's day when the kitchen feels like an oven. But even when the temperature is "just right," an outdoor barbecue area is an ideal place for informal gatherings and meals with family and friends. Whether built into a section of the deck or positioned nearby, a barbecue/cooking center functions best when it isn't too far from the house—transporting dishes and foods can be tiresome—but not so close that smoke and odors can drift indoors. It's also wise to place the barbecue a distance from overhanging limbs. This will prevent heat damage to leaves and assist in fire safety.

Simple kettle-style units that use charcoal briquets and built-in masonry designs work perfectly well, but gas-fueled barbecues have become popular alternatives. Regardless of the equipment, though, augmenting the cooking area with counters, shelving, storage, and perhaps even a sink can be a real bonus for frequent entertaining. Even if a deck plan can't accommodate a mini kitchen, setting aside an area for storing essentials, such as charcoal and utensils, can make cooking outdoors a breeze.

EASY COOKING

This compact cooking area at the side of the deck (left) puts work and storage space right at the chef's fingertips. Shielded from the wind and sun, the recessed counter doubles as a serving area. The open-face gas barbecue is designed to vent smoke up and away from seating and spa areas. Design: Dennis' Seven Dees Landscaping. ACQ-treated Douglas fir deck: J.H. Baxter & Company.

SPACE-SAVER

Almost as close to a kitchen as can be found outdoors, this tile-topped cooking center (above) packs plenty of storage and work space into a step-saving angled design. Its location—near the dining areas of the deck but not in their midst—allows several cooks to work at once and still be part of the party. Gas barbecue and accessories: Robert H. Peterson Co.

ENTERTAINING MADE EASY

A highlight of a multilevel deck design (above) that's geared for entertaining, this redwood wet bar is pleasing to the eye and practical to use. Behind its doors are shelves for glasses and bar accessories and storage for cooking utensils. The small barbecue on the tile counter is perfect for grilling snacks and hors d'oeuvres.

STYLISH SUPPORTS FOR PLANTS

One of the most familiar, attractive, and practical structures for supporting plants on and around the deck, the trellis needs little introduction. Usually constructed of thin wood strips nailed together in an open-weave or lattice design, trellises display a fairly slender profile. They may be attached to a wall, stand alone on a sturdy base, or be used overhead as both a support for climbing vines and a sunshade. Trellises can also serve as privacy screens or simple, inexpensive fencing to camouflage a utilitarian sideyard or divert attention from an unsightly view.

Arbors, too, are usually constructed from wood and serve as plant supports. Unlike a trellis, though, an arbor is a freestanding garden structure with space beneath to walk, sit, or simply tend to shade-loving plants. An arbor covered with grapes or blackberries can be a welcome companion to a vegetable or flower garden and a delightful place to bring adults and children together to harvest fruit.

RUSTIC SUPPORT

This rustic arbor (below), aged with time, easily supports a tangle of vines and shades the flowers and ground below. Through the framework of mossy limbs are glimpses of a manicured landscape, setting up a comfortable contrast.

SIMPLICITY IN THE GARDEN

The simple but versatile trellis (left) can suit a number of garden needs. Here, it supports climbing vines, obscures a neighboring house, and creates an inviting corner to tend flowers.

A romantic marriage of arbor and trellis, this style of garden structure (left) can suit many traditional settings. Climbing roses fill the space with beauty, color, and fragrance. The simply detailed design includes built-in benches to encourage a prolonged stay.

SHADE COVERINGS SOFTEN THE SUN

SUN OR SHADE

A striped awning (above) lends a festive note to the brick and wood facade, suiting the color and style of the house. The covering provides ample shade for the deck as well as a dry place to sit during summer showers. When the sun's warmth is welcome, the awning retracts into a housing with a shallow profile. Design and construction: Archadeck.

Without overhead shade, sunnyside decks can be unbearably hot during summer months, and if they sit close to the house, they can reflect heat into the interior. Unless the deck has large leafy trees nearby or an overhanging roof, some kind of covering or shelter is needed to spell relief.

A shade structure should be designed to moderate the sun's rays without blocking light, air, or desirable views from the deck. It should also be compatible with the style of the house and the size and scale of the deck it shelters. Most overhead screens are constructed of wood—boards, slats, or latticework—but they can also be fashioned from other materials such as bamboo or reeds. Canvas awnings and translucent plastic are also good choices when the elements—rain as well as sun—interfere with enjoying a deck.

Overhead shelters can also serve as privacy screens, obscuring views from rooms above or a building next door. When boards are closely spaced or covered with a vine, the deck below can feel as enclosed and inviting as an indoor room.

FULL-LENGTH SHADE

Stretching the length of this festive deck, an overhead shelter (left) shades the entire house wall and protects greenery that would otherwise bake in the sun. The narrow spacing of the wood slats creates a roof effect while allowing light to spill through. Design and construction: Yankee Barn Homes.

POINT OF INTEREST

A focal point at the edge of the deck, this bold shade structure (right) draws people to its seating area and creates a sense of enclosure without hemming them in. The open-weave vertical screens and strong horizontal lines set up an interesting light and shadow display on the patterned deck floor. Design: J.P. Franzen Assoc.

REDWOOD BEAUTY

The showpiece of this handsome deck, a beautifully crafted pergola (right) gives definition to the sunken Japanese-style firepit at its feet. Inspired by the Craftsman-style architecture, the all-redwood design features a roof of stacked timbers that's softened by a shade-casting lattice grille and built-in planters.

OVERHEAD DRAMA FOR DECK DESIGNS

In essence an arbor with an open roof, a pergola can give presence to a part of a deck or garden that lacks visual interest or highlight a special feature such as a spa or conversation area. The rafters and crosspieces that are so prominent in many pergola designs can also add height and mass to an otherwise flat portion of the deck. Often, pergolas are intended to serve strictly as decorative or architectural elements in a deck design. With a few minor changes to the open roof system, though, and perhaps the addition of a climbing vine or two, a pergola can become a dramatic overhead shelter.

A pergola can also employ a series of separate vertical structures tied together visually with a band of horizontal boards at the top. This elongated design works well to unify different areas of a deck, delineate a walkway, or give an impression of a roofed passageway from one part of the garden to another. When laced with greenery overhead, it can take on the feeling of an arbor.

OVERHEAD EMBRACE

Narrow boards and an open framework give this pergola (above) a light feeling that suits its role as a spa shelter. Its broad, gently angled design seems to embrace the spa without overwhelming it or the deck. Pressure-treated lumber: Wolmanized Lumber.

UNIFIED STYLE

As it travels across a portion of this well-equipped deck, the pergola (left) ties together the area's amenities and provides a measure of shade. Design: Dennis' Seven Dees Landscaping. ACQ-treated Douglas fir deck: J.H. Baxter & Company.

GAZEBOS EVOKE PAST PLEASURES

Set well apart from deckside activities but visually connected with all its surroundings, this gazebo (below) serves as a relaxing retreat. The octagonal shape, white-paint finish, and rooftop lantern for admitting light and air are typical Victorian-style features. Design and construction: Archadeck.

At the height of its popularity in Victorian times, the gazebo was an airy summerhouse or gar-den structure set well away from the main house, often on a knoll where views were especially pleasant. As was the fashion, they were elaborately styled and embellished with intricate fretwork. Today's gazebos fulfill the same function, providing an open-air retreat. Although most modern gazebos are more simply styled than their predecessors, they often have the same traditional octagonal shape, turreted roof, and decorative detailing.

As a structure to complement both home and garden, a gazebo can serve as more than an attractive focal point or seating with a view. It might function as a children's play space or a charming spot for Sunday brunch. Partially enclosed, it could act as a poolside changing room, a studio, or a storage area for garden tools. However it suits your particular needs, a gazebo can bring old-fashioned pleasure to the yard.

A spa surround with charm, this sheltered corner recalls another type of gazebo from yesteryear—a turreted balcony perched on the side of a building (right). Spa design and construction: Prestige Pools.

DETAILS MAKE A DIFFERENCE

A basic deck becomes more functional and interesting with amenities such as a spa or overhead shelter, and it gains additional appeal when attention is given to details. A railing that follows a curving path takes the eye smoothly around the deck, bringing continuity to the design. Comfortable seating built into the deck helps unify the area and doesn't take up valuable space that might be designated for other uses. Customized stairs can do more than lead up and down, they can serve as decorative elements as well as transition points. Planters and tree surrounds bring a bit of the landscape directly to the deck, adding color and texture. A firepit offers warmth and encourages friendly conversations. A well-thought-out lighting plan can bring drama and beauty to the entire area while extending the deck's use into the evening. Even small details such as varying the pattern of the floorboards, improving the workmanship of railings and benches, and coordinating finishes and colors can make a noticeable difference.

This chapter covers a few of the many custom touches that can enhance a deck's appearance and add to the enjoyment of outdoor living.

GRACEFUL LINES

The finishing touch to this redwood deck in the trees (right) is a curvilinear railing that wraps gracefully around the entire area. The opening between the horizontal rails is a thoughtful detail that allows those seated to view the natural scenery more easily.

SAFETY WITH A CUSTOM TOUCH

For decks that are elevated more than a few feet above the ground, railings are essential safety features. They are also one of the more prominent elements in a deck plan and lend themselves to custom treatments that can enhance the entire design.

Although the familiar crib-style railing has great appeal for its basic, simple lines and straightforward construction, it can take on custom effects with a few variations. Narrow tubular piping can replace the stringers between posts, for example, or the balusters (the vertical portions of the rail) can stop short of their usual height, leaving an opening below the topmost horizontal railing, or cap, to provide more open views when seated. If unobstructed views are the primary goal, the railing design can incorporate plexiglass inserts, stainless steel cable, or wire mesh screening (welded fabric)—all safe, contemporary alternatives to traditional railings. If more privacy or less street noise is required, the railing can take the form of a solid half-wall or low lattice fence, perhaps topped with planters. With a little planning and imagination, the choices are endless.

GENTLE CURVES

The elegant sweep of this railing (above) as it follows the veranda's curved edge was influenced in part by the contours of the site and also by its location adjacent to a music room. Here, the shape echoes that of a grand piano. The stained redwood balusters, gently curved on both sides, soften the design and contrast nicely with the weathered floor. The space beneath the deck is used for storing wood. Design: Lydia Strauss-Edwards.

CUSTOM DESIGN

The attractive splayed pattern and light natural finish of this railing design (above) are perfect complements to the traditionally styled house. Space-saving benches and planters rimming the deck open up the central area to a variety of uses and ease access to the backyard. Design and construction: Archadeck.

CRAFTSMAN THEME

Fluid lines and a light yet secure look give this redwood railing (right) extra eye-catching appeal. The workmanship and detailing that characterize the design—curved laminated horizontal rails, beveled edges, and rounded post and spindle tops—demonstrate the Craftsman theme of using wood expressively.

PRACTICAL, PLEASING BENCHES

Every deck needs a place or two for sitting, whether to read, relax after a long day, or chat with friends. And though a grouping of chairs can do the job nicely, built-in wood benches provide an alternative that suits the look and mood of a deck. Built-in benches also consume less space, and when positioned along the perimeter, they can free up portions of the deck for other activities. These practical accents can be used as focal points to show off an unusual design or beautiful crafting. Or they can be styled to blend in quietly, allowing some other feature to take center stage. Since built-in benches can't be pushed in or out of the sun, careful consideration should be given to their location. A good solution might be to position the benches strategically in areas that receive both sun and shade at different times of the day.

A well-designed bench is comfortable and roomy enough for two people to sit. If it isn't deep enough, it will feel like a perch rather than a seat. A long, deeper-than-usual bench can serve as a platform for sunbathing and, with cushions, makes a great place to stretch out for a nap.

DOUBLE-DUTY

As a deck accent, this bench-with-a-difference (above) has plenty to offer. Its wraparound seat and slatted backrest double as the base for a handy serving buffet. The bench also sits at just the right height for kids to reach the counter to get their own drinks and snacks. Design: Neil Kelly Designers/Remodelers. CCA-treated hem-fir deck: McFarland Cascade.

MATCHING FEATURES

The curved back piece and lattice-filled armrests of this inviting redwood bench (left) echo the design of the redwood structure overhead. The well-proportioned seat also integrates smoothly with the adjoining railings. Built into the deck perimeter, the bench lies near the activities but out of the path of foot traffic. Design and construction: Bryan Hays.

DISTINCT STYLE

This Colonial Williamsburg setting called for a rustic wood bench (left) that's as unusual as it is charming. Both a bench and a bridge, this inviting seat encourages a moment's pause on the path from one part of the garden to another.

WARM GATHERING PLACES

Unlike stairs and railings, essential ingredients for most decks, a firepit is an accent that's meant for pure enjoyment of the outdoor space. Like a campfire in the woods or on the beach that serves to warm hands and feet and stimulate friendly conversation among those gathered 'round, the firepit brings warmth and conversation closer to home. A firepit can be especially welcome when evenings turn cool or days become brisk, extending the life of the deck as an outdoor room.

Firepits are often situated on a patch of ground near the deck and its activities. When integrated directly into the deck design, however, firepits require some careful planning. Because of their weight and also as a safety measure, the base should sit directly on the ground. This works best with on-grade decks; with a raised deck, the base can be built up to the desired height using concrete blocks or masonry materials. A firepit should also be lined with heat-resistant firebrick, although a more decorative brick or natural stone can be used for the edging or trim. Finally, the sides of the firepit should be tall enough so that the surrounding deck boards will not be damaged or scorched by the fire. An alternative to a masonry firepit is a freestanding, metal woodburner. Often dish-shaped, it stands on legs and can be set on a protected surface.

INTIMATE STYLE

Encircled by an intimate conversation area, the brick-edged firepit (right) is the focal point of the lower deck yet lies just a few steps below the sheltered spa. The curved redwood bench allows everyone seated to enjoy the fire's warmth while the built-in backrest and planters bring a cozy feeling and privacy to the space. Design and construction: Timothy R. Bitts, Sun Wave Construction.

LOW-LEVEL WARMTH

Following the gentle slope in a series of broad platforms, this deck incorporates a brick firepit (left) into its lowest level. The zigzag pattern of floorboards and planters adds visual interest on the path from the shade pavilion to the lounging area around the firepit.

TIME-HONORED LOOK

Aged to perfection, these oaks grew here long before the house and its secluded oriental garden came into being. The simple platform deck (right) respects the trees' presence and offers a sure-footed path through the landscape.

EMBRACING TREES WITH A SURROUND

Trees have a special place in the home landscape, supplying privacy, shade, and wind protection while adding color, texture, and natural beauty. Displacing mature trees to make room for an outdoor living area may solve one problem but create another. Fortunately, the flexibility of wood decks to adapt to a variety of sites provides the option of including trees in their design. Unlike many patios, decks can closely surround a tree without interfering with the root system or cutting off its supply of air and water. The opening around the trunk, however, should be large enough to allow for continued growth, especially if the tree is young or a rapid grower.

Benches and tree surrounds seem meant for each other, whether separate benches sit close to the base or a single seat wraps itself all the way around. The surround can also take the form of a low wall elevated above the deck floor, wide enough for comfortable sitting and often tall enough to double as a railing filled with shade-loving flowers and small-scale shrubs—as long as they and the tree require the same soil and water conditions.

ROOM TO GROW

A small tree finds a home in a deck surround (above) that's sized to allow unhindered growth. Integrated beautifully with the house and surrounding deck in color, style, and material, the thoughtfully designed enclosure incorporates a planter/bench for informal sitting.

FUNCTIONAL DETAILS

This spacious deck (right) incorporates a tree surround designed to echo nearby railings and sized to accommodate a growing trunk. Raised above the ground to capture woodland views, the deck provides ample built-in seating on two levels and plenty of floor space to set up extra tables and chairs. Water repellent finish: Wolman Wood Care Products.

COLORFUL ACCENTS FOR THE DECK

As rewarding and versatile as a deck can be, sometimes its expanse of wood needs a splash of color to liven things up. Planters, built-in or standing free, are among the easiest—and least expensive—ways to dress up a deck and tie it in visually to the house and the rest of the landscape. Planters may be incorporated into a railing design at the top of a post, a column connecting sections, or as part of the railing itself. On a deck that sits close to the ground, planters can be grouped to follow the edge and give the area definition. They can be positioned to mark a stairway, denote a change in levels, and divide the deck into zones. On-grade decks can use the planter theme in yet another way, with openings cut into the deck floor to accommodate plants and allow them to root directly in the ground.

Planters bring more than color to a deck. With proper drainage and a little attention, annual and perennial flowers can provide fragrance and blooms over a long period. Vegetables and fruits that grow well in contained spaces, such as cherry tomatoes, peppers, and strawberries, can supply a bit of fresh summer produce. Even in winter, small berry-producing shrubs in a planter can add seasonal color and cheer.

A PRACTICAL ADDITION

These straightforward planter boxes (above) have no fancy airs, but they do their job as barriers to keep deck users back from the edge. The open area beneath the boxes helps prevent rot by allowing water to drain away from the planter and deck boards and by allowing air to circulate between surfaces. Pressure-treated lumber: Georgia Pacific Corp.

PLANTERS WITH A PURPOSE

A highlight of this functional, multipurpose redwood deck, these planter boxes (right) were lined with tin to minimize the wood's contact with soil and water. Glazed ceramic tile strips accenting the planters add a lively note, bringing a splash of color to the deck. Design: John Hemingway.

CONTAINED BEAUTY

A variety of shapes and forms brings visual interest to a series of redwood platforms connecting different levels of this hillside deck (above). An extensive redwood retaining wall keeps the rocky slope at bay and gives an impression of a large built-in planter.

BENEFICIAL BUILT-IN PLANTERS

Built-in planters can be a small deck's best friend, especially when paired with built-in seating and kept in scale with the small size of the area. They can be clustered in a space-saving group at one side of the deck or at changes in levels to provide additional open space and improve traffic flow. A planter wall can be designed as a backrest for a bench; its cap can also double as an im-

promptu shelf for setting down plates and glasses. Of course, large decks can benefit from planters, too, often without the restrictions imposed by a smaller area. Large planters can be particularly useful as privacy screens when filled with tall or bushy plants or when combined with a vertical trellis.

A planter of any shape or size should be constructed from wood that's resistant to decay and retains its good looks over time. Redwood, among a handful of other species, is a popular choice for many deck projects. It's important, however, to select the proper grade of lumber for the job. Heartwood, which is cut from the center of the tree, is strong and naturally resistant to rot that can develop when wood comes in contact with water and soil. Any grade that includes "heart" in its name, such as construction heart or all-heart, is an ideal material for planters.

DESIGNED TO PLEASE

This small but functional corner of a larger deck (left) relies on built-in planters and benches to give one wing of the house its own outdoor space. The eye-pleasing redwood deck covers a former patio area that was composed of a patchwork of crumbling concrete, loose bricks, and weed-filled grass. Design: Mark Becker.

POINT OF INTEREST

A handsome, colorful barrier at the far end of a spacious redwood deck that stands high off the ground, this large planter (right) helps screen views of neighboring houses. An overhead trellis eases the visual transition between the deck railing and the house. Constructed from all-heart redwood, the planter is coated with a water repellent to help maintain the wood's natural hue.

ACCENT ON DECK LIGHTING

Nighttime activities on the deck require good lighting to assist with tasks such as cooking and dining, to make socializing more pleasurable, and to increase safety, especially on stairs and at level changes. Often, exterior house lights will do the job, especially if the deck lies close to the building; but for aesthetics and maximum enjoyment, lighting specifically designed for the deck is a detail worth having.

On the deck, patio, or anywhere outdoors, low-voltage lighting is the recommended system. It's safe—even wet or bare wires won't give off a shock—economical to run, and relatively easy to install. Furthermore, there are a number of choices among low-voltage fixtures that can suit any style deck. Surface/deck lights, for instance, are low-profile fixtures that can be attached horizontally or vertically to a wood surface such as a railing, step, planter box, or bench. Tier lights, which spread light evenly around a given area, can be mounted strategically on the deck floor, at the top and bottom of stairs, and near seating to illuminate the overall space. Floodlights can be used in combination with other lighting to highlight a feature of the deck design, such as the pool or spa, or tie the deck area to the surrounding yard. In fact, like the versatile decks they illuminate, outdoor lighting offers endless possibilities.

SPACE-SAVING FEATURE

A seaside deck's stairway (above) adopts a nautical air with low-voltage surface fixtures. These deck lights take up minimal space yet offer plenty of light for safe passage. Deck lights: Intermatic, Inc.

LIGHT UP THE NIGHT

Thanks to well-designed lighting, this dramatic redwood deck (left) offers as much use at night as it does by day. The deck features a lighting system that's incorporated into the lattice-screened storage area underneath. Globe fixtures shed light in all directions, illuminating the nearby woods as well as the deck.

BRILLIANT ACCENTS

These multiuse, low-voltage lights can be used all around the deck (right)—they cast a gentle glow on flowering shrubs from the railing. Measuring only 3½" × 3¼", the compact redwood fixtures can be stained to match surrounding wood or left to weather to a pale finish. Deck lights: The Toro Company.

PAVINGS FOR THE PATIO

As functional and pleasing areas for outdoor living, patios have unlimited potential. Unlike decks, which are limited to primarily wood construction, patios have a number of options among masonry materials. In fact, the material they're fashioned from gives patios and walkways their supreme durability and traditional good looks.

A patio might be paved with natural stone such as quarried flagstone or smoothed river rock. Rougher stones can also be cut and shaped to serve as pavers and edgings. Brick has always been high on the list of desirable materials thanks to its widespread availability, uniform size, and ease of installation. Ceramic tile is another option, and when colored in warm, earthy tones, it looks terrific outdoors. Versatile poured concrete is a long-lasting, economical alternative to other materials. Its surface can be dressed up with aggregates or a variety of embossed, colored finishes. Concrete also comes in all manner of pavers that can be used individually or interconnected to form a stable surface. And combining different forms of masonry in thoughtful ways can add visual interest to the patio and its surroundings.

A NATURAL BLEND

Thoroughly inviting, even after a summer shower, this terraced patio (right) deftly integrates several natural materials into its design: flagstone flooring, fieldstone walls, and wood fencing. Contained by rustic walls and an English-style perennial garden, the patio has a secluded, tranquil feeling. Design: Carter Van Dyke Assoc.

NATURAL STONE FOR LASTING BEAUTY

Durable, beautiful natural stone is a patio material that can last almost forever, and flagstone has long been a favorite for its versatility and interesting visual character. Flagstone belongs to a class of stone called ashlar that is quarried from mountainsides and usually cut and shaped at the work site into relatively thin pieces with squared edges. Other quarried stone that can be used for patios and walkways includes sandstone, slate, limestone, and granite. Fieldstone, on the other hand, is gathered from streams, riverbeds, and open fields and typically has an irregular shape and rougher surface. In its natural form, most fieldstone works best in walls and as an edging, but when custom cut into a smoother shape, it can make a fine patio floor.

Flagstone patios fashioned from rectangular-cut stones of a similar size and color have a neat yet natural appearance that integrates nicely with a variety of house styles and landscape designs. Flagstone also blends graciously with other natural materials such as fieldstone, wood, and virtually any plantings found in the garden.

LONG-LASTING STONE

This inviting flagstone patio (above) located in a shady corner of the garden shows the lasting quality of a material that grows more beautiful with time. Stone benches at the base of the vine-covered tree underscore the natural setting.

FORMAL LAYOUT

An orderly pattern of flagstone rectangles gives structure and a bit of formality to this patio and pool surround (right). Natural variations in color add visual interest to the expansive patio area and blend well with the colors of the house and the outdoor furnishings.

THE BEAUTY OF NATURAL STONE

Fallen leaves and an autumn mist lend a special look to this flagstone patio (above), which is contained on one side by a curved fieldstone wall and, closer in, a rustic wood fence. Wet flagstone often displays a beautiful sheen that highlights its surface. Design: Carter Van Dyke Assoc.

Closely set but randomly laid, these flagstones blend together to create a subtly colored, slightly uniform surface that suits this secluded patio retreat (left). Mossy joints between the stones and the mature surrounding landscape suggest that this patio has aged gracefully with time.

FLAGSTONE TAKES A RANDOM PATH

Unlike some patio materials, flagstone can be laid in a free-flowing random pattern that intermixes natural color, texture, and line in interesting ways. Similar shades of color and roughly the same size stones can create a subtle, informal, and fairly consistent look. By contrast, flagstones selected for their unusual shapes, rich hues, or contrasting surface textures can be laid in random patterns that range in appearance from lively patchwork designs—sometimes called "crazy paving"—to thoughtful combinations intended to showcase the materials themselves. Flagstones can range in color from creamy beige to pinkish-tan to terra cotta and from gray to purplish-brown to dark chocolate.

Constructing a flagstone patio or walk is a fairly simple matter. As long as the soil base is level and stable, the stones can be laid directly on the ground. (Very thin flagstone, or veneer, requires a concrete slab base.) When stones are set close together, sand can be brushed over them to fill the grooves and discourage weeds at the same time. Set further apart with topsoil in between, flagstones can be edged with grass or a ground cover to soften their appearance and cushion the hardness underfoot.

DISTINCT DESIGN

With its random patchwork effect and close-knit design, this small flagstone patio (left) is a lively contrast to the surrounding country garden. At one side of the gazebo, a waterfall cascades down a man-made streambed of natural fieldstone. Laying broken flagstone in a jigsawlike pattern such as this one takes time and patience. Design: The Brickman Group.

GRACIOUS, TRADITIONAL BRICK

For a patio or walkway that requires a gracious, traditional look, brick is an excellent choice. It's attractive, practical, and durable and provides even a new patio with a sense of permanence. Brick's uniform shape and size make it a wonderful candidate for all kinds of creative patterns, too. It works beautifully in combination with other materials such as railroad ties, redwood, natural stone, and concrete. And with its range of earth-tone colors in both new and old pavers, brick can complement and enhance nearly any style house.

Devising just the right pattern for a brick patio is a relatively easy matter because the bricks can be easily handled and grouped before they're actually installed—a definite advantage over a material such as poured concrete. There are several brick patterns that are traditional favorites, including herringbone, basket weave, and a variety of straight and diagonal runs. Curving and circular patterns are more challenging to plan but can lend a softness to the patio that's a pleasing change of pace from rectilinear designs.

DURABLE FEATURE

Chipped and worn with time, the rustic yet rich look of these bricks (left) testifies to the material's lasting beauty. After years of foot traffic, the herringbone pattern remains intact.

SATISFYING RESULTS

The zigzag design of the herringbone pattern (right) is more difficult to achieve than a straight run, but the neat angular effect is worth the effort. The angled pattern also prevents the bricks from moving when they are laid in sand.

CREATIVE PATTERN

Brick laid in a herringbone pattern is the focal point of this patio (right). Variations in brick color add visual interest. The wide mortared joints and a smooth surface suggest that the brick was laid on a concrete slab or over an existing patio. Design: Powell Design Group, Inc.

LIVING OUTDOORS WITH BRICK

Of the many choices available in the world of brick, the two types recommended for patio construction are common, or building, brick and paving brick. Common brick can be used for basically any outdoor project, and the slight variations in color and texture from one brick to another can give a patio or walkway character and add to its appeal. Common brick may be new, used, or newly made and treated to look old or used. Paving brick, formed from a special clay and fired for a long period, is very hard and makes a good selection for patios or driveways that will endure heavy traffic.

Brick's design flexibility and lasting good looks as a paving material are joined by another positive feature: ease of installation. Most brick patios can be laid on a bed of sand as long as the soil base is stable, the bricks are butted tightly together, and some kind of solid edging is employed to keep the bricks from creeping or spreading apart. Of course, some site conditions require a stronger base for safety and stability. In these situations, the brick is usually laid on a concrete slab with mortared joints.

A SECURE BASE

This brick walkway (above) displays a variation of the basket-weave pattern. The bricks along the grassy area have sturdy mortared joints to offset the spreading motion seen within the informally laid walk. Brick: Redland Brick, Inc.

A RUSTIC BLEND

The subdued but varied coloration of these brick pavers (right) is suggestive of natural stone and contributes to the relaxing atmosphere of this inviting outdoor space. The bricks' earth tones blend harmoniously with the fieldstone encircling the little lily pond.

LASTING BEAUTY

A larger view of this patio (right) shows the layout of the brick pavers. They were laid on a sand base in a popular pattern known as running bond, which is often seen in brick walls. Bricks set vertically on edge border the patio and help keep the pavers from moving.

OLD-WORLD ELEGANCE

As an entree to a dramatic neoclassic home, this elegant curving driveway (above) features prestained concrete pavers with a cobblestone theme. Authentic-looking reminders of traditional paving materials, these precast stones are more affordable, readily available alternatives to natural-cut stone. Design: Tyler Gazecki.

GREAT POSSIBILITIES WITH PAVERS

There was a time when the only concrete pavers available were rectangular blocks, which are sturdy but often uninteresting solutions for walkways and patios. Today, precast concrete pavers can be found in dozens of shapes, sizes, and colors and serve as surprisingly realistic substitutes for brick, cobblestone, tile, and even granite. In addition to the familiar squares and circles, pavers come in a variety of more interesting shapes such as hexagons, diamonds, and free-form designs that can be creatively arranged to bring a patio to life.

Interlocking pavers—units that fit together like pieces of a puzzle—are manufactured from a dense form of concrete, and most products are exceptionally strong. When joined together, interlocking pavers create a rigid, fairly smooth surface that stays in alignment even when laid in sand, making it ideal for areas that sustain a lot of foot traffic. Interlocking pavers can also be used in places that bear heavier loads than most materials can handle, including driveways.

A PRACTICAL SUBSTITUTE

These attractive, natural-looking pavers (above) are constructed from a manufactured product that simulates the colors, textures, and shapes found in natural stone. The synthetic rock edging the area is much lighter in weight than true stone and also more economical to buy and install. Pavers: Stone Products Corp.

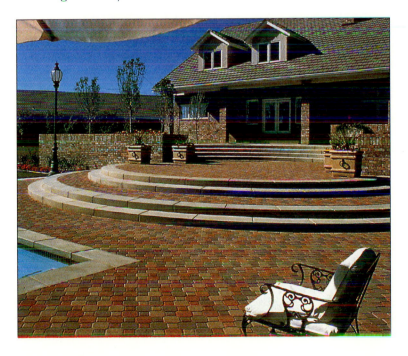

SIMPLE CONNECTION

Echoing the textures and colors of the brick facade of the house and its adjoining privacy wall (left), these bricklike pavers bring continuity to the terraced patio and provide a stable surface that supports all kinds of outdoor activities. The semicircular levels descending to the pool help soften the large expanse of stonelike materials.

PRECUT AND PRECAST PATIO STONE

Stone materials such as precut concrete block and formed-in-place concrete may not look quite as natural as true stone, but they perform admirably as smooth, even surfaces for patios and walkways. Unlike a great expanse of poured concrete, smaller units and sections offer design flexibility and lend themselves to both formal and informal patterns. They can be positioned close together in a tight grid, for instance, and separated by thin redwood timbers, a line of bricks, or a strip of ceramic tile. For a softer, more casual appearance, they can be laid randomly or distanced farther apart with grass or a ground cover filling the gaps.

Several types of natural stone can also be found precut into rectangular shapes. Sometimes referred to as stone tiles, they are substantially more costly than concrete, especially if they have been "dressed"—cut to a specific size and thickness or custom cut for a particular project. Stone block is usually less finished than stone tile, with its corners squared but not perfect, the edges only roughly parallel, and its surface a bit rugged underfoot.

RUGGED BEAUTY

This natural stone (above) has been cut into a shape called Belgian block and is frequently laid in bricklike patterns. It also blends gracefully with other materials. An old millstone commands attention at the patio edge.

REFINED TEXTURE

Neatly fashioned into a rectangular design, these crisp-edged concrete blocks (right) were carefully cast in place on the patio floor. Small smooth river rocks, similarly colored and sized, create a contrasting border between the stones.

CASUAL CHARM

An orderly procession of precast, precut concrete squares marches across this eye-pleasing patio (above). Several types of creeping ground cover spill their leaves over the blocks, softening the patio's look and providing a more resilient walking surface.

UNIQUE DESIGN

An unusual pattern of cobblestone and old brick swirls its way across a section of this patio (left). While not perfectly squared or smooth, cobblestone is a cut stone that has been used in patios, walkways, and streets for centuries.

FIELDSTONE COMES TO THE PATIO

Simply described, fieldstone refers to nearly any kind of stone commonly found in fields, foothills, and along river banks and streambeds. This plentiful natural material is all the more interesting because its composition—color, texture, and shape—varies widely from region to region. In its "found" state, fieldstone can be rough and oddly shaped, which is fine for rustic walls but not particularly suited to patios. The best choices are usually stone that's been cut or broken into smaller, thinner pieces and river rock that's naturally worn and smooth. For comfort and safety, it's wise to select stones that have at least one flat side to serve as the patio surface.

Like flagstone, fieldstone can be arranged into countless patterns and designs—random and otherwise—and laid in sand on a stable base. And like so many of its companion materials, it can stand on its own or be incorporated into a patio design as an accent or detail.

SECURE ARRANGEMENT

Clustered in a grouping of similar-size pavers, these rounded stones (right) were wedged close together for a more uniform effect.

INTRICATE PATTERN

Deceptively simple in appearance, this mosaic of irregular stone (above) was artfully and painstakingly composed in a close-knit design that provides a firm surface underfoot.

CHANGE OF PACE

Framed by a profusion of multicolored plantings, this oceanside patio (left) exhibits a lively color and rich texture of its own. Informally arranged in sand, the individual fieldstones have a slightly uneven surface that calls for leisurely walking rather than a quick pace.

SMOOTH CROSSING

Set casually in a gravel bed, these angular fieldstones (right) were laid with their flat side exposed to permit easier passage across the patio.

DECORATIVE FINISH FOR CONCRETE

Although plain white concrete offers clean, uncomplicated looks and suits a host of patio styles, it sometimes needs a little extra attention to improve its visual appeal. An exposed aggregate finish is one of the simplest and most practical ways to dress up concrete, giving it a pebbled appearance and adding texture underfoot.

Fine and coarse aggregates such as sand and gravel are part of the ingredients that go into the making of concrete, along with cement and water. Typically, the aggregates are integral to the mixture and not especially noticeable when the concrete dries. Exposed aggregate refers to a decorative finish in which small rounded pebbles, naturally-colored gravels, or crushed stone are embedded, or seeded, into the surface of fresh concrete. Although some finishes incorporate larger stones and use different techniques, the end result is a rugged slip-resistant, easy-to-maintain surface.

An exposed aggregate patio or walkway looks especially attractive when broken into smaller segments and combined with a contrasting material, such as brick, wood, or tile. And when the accent material carries into planters and walls, the overall effect can be quite pleasing.

VISUAL APPEAL

So-called seeded aggregate is a popular concrete finish (above). The pebbled texture adds visual interest, helps cut glare, and provides a slip-resistant surface when wet, which makes it ideal for walkways and around pools.

NAUTICAL MOOD

Like pebbles clustered on a beach, this mosaic of smooth oval river stones set in white concrete reflects the colors and mood of this patio's seaside setting (left). The weathered redwood timbers framing the exposed aggregate squares add to the charm of this lively patio. Landscape design: John Summers and Patrick Murphy.

PLEASING COMBINATION

The patio's finish is tailored to complement the materials and architectural detailing of this home (above), which features a hybrid design reflecting Craftsman and prairie styles. The exposed aggregate and brick walkway blend comfortably with the colors and textures of soil and shrubbery. The well-defined brickwork continues up the front stairs.

INFORMAL TERRA COTTA TILE

Of the vast numbers of ceramic tile available for house and garden, terra cotta tiles are perhaps the most widely selected for outdoor use. The term terra cotta, meaning baked earth in Italian, typically refers to rather rustic-looking tiles that are colored in warm, earthy, and natural tones. Within the terra cotta family, however, there are several types of tile—some glazed, some unglazed, and all with slightly different characteristics.

Hand-molded, unglazed tiles, sometimes called Mexican pavers, usually have an uneven surface and a handcrafted look. And while their informal, rustic appearance rates high, they are soft and porous and should be sealed to reduce water absorption. Unglazed pavers are also apt to deteriorate in cold climates. Machine-made terra cotta tiles, commonly called quarry tiles, tend to be harder and more durable and may be found in glazed and unglazed forms in a variety of shapes and sizes. Most glazed tiles have a smooth finish and resist stains beautifully, but a too-smooth glazed surface can be slippery when wet.

WARM TONES

Brick-look quarry tiles laid in a herringbone pattern add dimension and visual interest to a terrace edging a rustic country house (right). These machine-made terra cotta tiles were glazed at the factory to give them a hard, weather-proof, stain-resistant finish. Tile: Summitville Tiles, Inc.

HAND-CRAFTED LOOK

Worn, weathered, and filled with old-world charm, these hand-molded terra cotta pavers suit the look and mood of the traditional Spanish-style home and its patio (left). Wide grout lines between tiles underscore the hexagonal pattern and help compensate for the uneven edges typical of hand-made pavers.

LASTING IMPRESSIONS IN CONCRETE

Imprinted concrete is one of the newer techniques that can transform this versatile material into a stone look-alike. With any number of patterns and seemingly endless color variations, imprinted, or embossed, concrete can be made to resemble a variety of patio materials such as new and used brick, formal slate, random-laid flagstone, terra cotta tile, cobblestones, and much more. As a patio paving, imprinted concrete is also an affordable way to give outdoor living areas a more natural look and bypass the time-consuming and sometimes costly process of selecting and laying individual bricks or stones.

Since it is a cast-concrete product—a concrete slab that's been integrally colored and then scored—this material can be used in areas that receive heavy traffic, such as driveways. It's also an ideal choice for pool surrounds and walkways since its textured surface is slip-resistant when wet.

SETTING A SOLID STYLE

Setting a patio style is both a matter of personal taste and an artful combination of materials to suit the house and site. On the one hand, a patio design should be influenced by lifestyle, family composition, and outdoor interests; on the other, it should incorporate materials with an eye to their intended function and their relationship to the house and surrounding landscape. If the patio is to be used for formal entertaining, for instance, a number of different pavings can be considered; but if the area will also be home to tricycles and other kids' play, the surface should be smooth yet slip-proof.

Because of their ground-level location, patios possess more design flexibility than decks. They can adopt nearly any shape, following the contours of the site or striking out on an individual course. They seldom require structural support and are therefore less costly to construct. Patios also enjoy a diverse choice of masonry materials, both natural and man-made, in countless colors and textures that can be used alone or in exciting combinations.

This chapter presents a portfolio of creative ways to bring masonry to life with shape, pattern, and a variety of stylish patio solutions.

DELIGHTFUL DETAILS

Enclosed by rugged boulders, a rustic fieldstone fireplace, and lush plantings, this sunken garden patio (right) is a visual and textural delight. The stacked stone steps and terraced flagstone floor follow the contours of the wooded site. Design: Robert W. Valleau.

UNIQUE CHARACTER OF FLAGSTONE

With its understated palette of browns and grays and an exceptional ability to blend comfortably into so many settings, flagstone remains one of the most desirable patio pavings. It seems especially suited to traditional homes and gardens—perhaps because of its natural rather than man-made origins—but it can also help soften the appearance of more contemporary houses and newly installed landscaping. Flagstone's slightly irregular surface displays a texture and warmth that complements virtually all plants, from mossy coverings between pavers to potted flowers to large-scale shrubs. For that reason, flagstone adapts easily to both formal and informal patios and walkways.

One feature that sets flagstone apart from some other materials is that every stone has an interesting face or an individual character. Even when cut into similar shapes or laid in a close pattern, each stone retains a unique quality that contributes to the overall patio's beauty.

MUTED SHADES AND COZY DINING

Breakfast al fresco takes on a romantic note in this shady, private corner of the patio (above). The simply styled teak furnishings suit the patio's small scale and harmonize with the soft gray shades of the flagstone floor.
Outdoor furniture: Gardenside, Ltd.

RICH TEXTURE

Lush surroundings and a garden brimming with color transform this simple rustic patio (right) into an inviting retreat. Informally laid in a random design, the large irregular stones show off their individual faces and colors.

A PEACEFUL COUNTRY FEELING

Years of accumulated moss give these bricks a time-worn look that suits the patio's rustic mood (above). The dark-toned bricks were laid in a traditional basket-weave design.

BRICK OF A DIFFERENT COLOR

AN EARTHY TONE

Laid in a neat herringbone pattern, this patio floor (below) carries the familiar orange color often associated with new bricks.

Suited to a host of house styles and patio configurations, brick has long been high on the list of favorite patio materials. And though the familiar image of this versatile paver brings to mind the color family of reds and yellows, brick is available in a wide range of dark, earthy tones, including black. These darker shades are usually formed during the firing process; the finished color is influenced by the type of clay and the amount of iron within the clay. Brick that's been streaked, or flashed, with dark lines also makes for an interesting patio surface.

A dark brick floor can give a patio an older, more traditional appearance and set up dramatic contrasts with lighter-colored elements such as furnishings and garden accents. It can also recede into the background, allowing foliage and flowers to take center stage.

CLASSIC ELEGANCE

The dressy effect of white on black brings formality outdoors to this enclosed patio (right). The black brick floor is an eye-pleasing foil to the traditionally styled furnishings and white house trim. Flowering shrubs inject splashes of color around the patio edge. Outdoor furniture: Brown Jordan Company.

WARM, MELLOW NATURAL TONES

PLEASING BACKDROP

The earthy terra cotta shades of this brick patio/courtyard (below) are a perfect background for the lush vegetation rimming the area. The large leafy plants give the enclosure the feeling of a secret garden. Festive red and white furnishings add a splash of color to the space.

While dark brick can offer interesting contrasts and a strong red brick can create a more vibrant atmosphere on the patio, it is the more mellow intermediate shades of terra cotta that seem most at home in the majority of informal outdoor settings. These rather neutral earthy colors can make a patio floor or walkway seem more natural, more welcoming—especially when the bricks are laid in sand. Their muted reds, yellows, and browns harmonize with many other materials found outside, from fieldstone walls and wood fences to almost every kind of native vegetation and landscape plantings. Terra cotta colored bricks also make a pleasing backdrop for brighter accents.

Regardless of color, brick's adaptability is one of its greatest assets. As a building and paving material, it's been around a long time; ancient Babylonians and Egyptians, old world Romans, and new world Indians all made plentiful use of sun-dried or fired clay bricks. Today, it remains well-liked, much-used, and as versatile as ever.

CASUAL CHARM

Mellowed by weather and the passage of time, this mossy brick patio (right) blends charmingly with its adjoining shingled cottage. When the gated Dutch-style door is closed, the inviting outdoor space becomes a secluded little courtyard. Design: Ronald Bricke & Assoc.

PAIRING BRICKS WITH PLANTINGS

One of brick's endearing qualities is its ability to retain personality and a distinctive appearance in all types of patio designs. It can stand on its own as the sole paving material or intermix comfortably with one or more other natural or man-made mediums—be it stone, concrete, wood, or tile.

Brick is especially pleasing when integrated into patio garden settings and paired with a variety of plantings. A design might take the form of a curving floor that wraps around trees and low shrubbery, including places to sit in the sun or shade. Or it might be conceived as a formal outdoor area characterized by a tailored patterned brick floor and contained by neatly clipped hedges and planters. By contrast, the patio brickwork might spread informally into the yard, meandering past flower beds and pausing at a bench en route to the vegetable garden.

One reason the blend of brick and greenery is so satisfying is that unlike the combination of two hard materials, such as brick and concrete, the presence of plants introduces a visual and textural softness that makes any outdoor area more inviting.

DELIGHTFUL BLEND

Pockets of greenery and a soft border of shrubs infuse this little brick patio (right) with great charm. Contained by brickwork laid in a running bond pattern, the three mini gardens display herbs at their prettiest and place them conveniently close at hand.

BRICKWORK TAKES TO CIRCLES

Like ripples in a pond, this circle of bricks spreads across the patio (left), radiating warmth and color in all directions. Symmetrically designed and positioned, the graceful trellis and its inviting seating area recall romantic garden hideaways of Victorian times. Design: Kagan Architects & Planners.

When considered as an individual unit, the small rectangular block that constitutes a standard brick gives little hint of its tremendous potential as a pattern-making material. But its uniform shape and workable size give brick a design flexibility that allows even a novice to achieve sophisticated results. With a little patience and a few "dry runs," straightforward patterns like the herringbone and basket weave can be mastered quite easily. Circular patterns are a bit more difficult to execute, but the beauty of a curving design can be worth the extra time and effort.

Circular themes have been long used in stonework. In a patio design, a circular arrangement of bricks can express several different themes. A large curving pattern that covers the patio floor, for instance, can give the whole area a feeling of continuity and balance. A circle surrounded by bricks set in a contrasting pattern or color might serve as a dramatic focal point. And a series of small curving designs can set up a subtle rhythm that adds visual interest.

The focal point of this circular patio (left), a filigreed wrought-iron bench doubles as a tree surround and injects a European note into the setting. Muted in color and mood, the bricks follow an understated circular path based on a running bond pattern.

STYLISH CONCRETE PAVERS

Following the patio perimeter, a light-colored wood bench (below) echoes the buff shades that appear in the pavers' design. The combination of concrete and wood—including the timber-edged portions of the patio—suits the informal layout of the outdoor area.

With a long history of commercial applications, precast concrete pavers have recently made their way into the home landscape as attractive, adaptable alternatives to brick, tile, and natural stone. Although the term "precast concrete" makes the material sound uncomfortably industrial, these pavers are available in colors, shapes, and sizes that can be creatively arranged into any number of patio designs, complementing virtually any house style. Just a sampling from the selection of precast concrete pavers reveals Spanish-style terra cotta tiles, "aged" brick for formal or traditional settings, rustic cobblestones for more casual patios, and flagstonelike pavers in naturalistic colors that can enhance both formal and informal designs.

Aside from their flexibility as paving materials, concrete pavers offer the strength and durability of poured concrete in a much simpler form. They can be laid individually or locked together on a level, stable sand base and—like brick—lend themselves to interesting patterns.

The mottled, earthy colors of this patio floor (right) harmonize perfectly with the existing trees and flowering shrubs of the landscape design. The hexagonal pattern of the concrete pavers serves as a subtle contrast to the rectangular bricks of the garden wall.

CONTRASTS CREATE INTEREST

A PLEASING EFFECT

Refreshing to the eye and touch, the gently spreading ground cover also brings contrasting color and texture to this flagstone floor (left). The uneven surface encourages a slower pace when crossing this area of the patio.

While most patios carry more or less a continuous surface, breaking up the area with small amounts of a contrasting material can create interesting effects. Instead of being placed in close proximity, individual pavers such as bricks and stones can be spaced farther apart and the gaps filled with grass or ground cover, gravel, crushed stone, or pebbles. For a more formal look, the spacing can be patterned on a grid or a design with regularity to its lines. Informal outdoor areas seem more at ease with random patterns and free-form designs.

There are, however, some disadvantages to relinquishing a continuous surface. The change in materials underfoot can mean slower, more careful passage, especially at night. Even a slightly uneven surface can make it difficult to position tables and chairs without an annoying wobble. One solution is to make one portion of the patio level and smooth to accommodate a seating and dining space and use the contrasting material in areas where there's less activity.

POINT OF INTEREST

The arresting geometrics and symmetrical design of this stone composition create an unusual focal point on this patio (left). Finely crushed gravel sets up a light-colored, light-textured contrast to the darker flagstone pavers.

TEXTURED, PEBBLED CONCRETE

With a decorative finish, a basic concrete patio can take on a new personality as well as a dressier appearance. Of the several surface treatments applied to concrete, a seeded aggregate finish is probably the most familiar and most frequently used. This process embeds small pebbles or smooth crushed rock into wet concrete, giving the surface a slight texture and a distinctive look. Aggregate finishes can be light or dark in color, according to the composition of the stone selected; they can be more or less textured, depending on the stone size and amount of material left exposed.

Its crisp, uncluttered appearance and uniform surface makes seeded aggregate a fine choice for patios designed to complement contemporary-styled homes. The classic pebbled finish provides visual interest without the interference of strong color or pattern, texture without roughness, and a level surface that's ideal for hosting all the activities that accompany a contemporary lifestyle.

DECORATIVE ACCENT

Even poured concrete, seen below with a subtle aggregate finish, can incorporate interesting details, as long as they're planned in advance. This patio accent blends broken stones—some set in mortar, others in soil—with delicate clumps of ground cover.
Design: John Herbst, Jr.

CLASSIC FINISH

The dramatic architecture of this spacious contemporary home (right) called for a patio design that would suit the mood and scale of the house without competing. The solution? An expansive, terraced concrete patio geared for multiple functions and finished with a simple, stylish seeded aggregate surface that's easy to maintain and slip-resistant.
Design: Alan Liddle.

WORLDLY STYLE

A Mediterranean mood prevails in this appealing indoor-outdoor patio setting (left). The delicate pattern of the Italian-made tile floor belies a hard-working surface that's strong, durable, and stain-resistant. Italian Ceramic Tile: Italian Trade Commission.

ELEGANT TILE, ITALIAN STYLE

Among the choices for a patio surfacing, there's nothing more elegant than dressy Italian ceramic tile. The polished, high-style appearance of so many Italian imports is a perfect complement to formal indoor-outdoor settings. And although these tiles can integrate smoothly with a number of house styles in a variety of locations, they seem especially suited to homes and patios found in warmer regions or those designed around a Mediterranean theme. Their light, bright finishes and decorative motifs make an attractive backdrop for garden accents with a southern European flair: wrought iron furnishings, hand-painted clay pots, and stone fountains and benches. And they are one of the few pavings that can travel seamlessly from indoor spaces to outside living areas without visual interruption.

Ceramic tile today benefits from sophisticated glazing and finishing techniques that make them extremely durable and easy to maintain. Like several other paving materials, however, tile can be slippery when wet. A number of tiles are available with textured and matte surfaces that provide better traction yet still offer sophisticated looks.

POLISHED LOOKS

Inspired by the grand patios and courtyards of Italian palazzos, or palaces, this dramatic patio (left) underscores the neoclassic styling of the surrounding house. The refined, upscale appearance of the patterned tile floor creates an elegant, spacious surface for formal entertaining. Design: Tyler Gazecki.

TILE WITH SUBSTANCE AND STYLE

Fashioned by hand or shaped by machine, informal terra cotta tiles bring warm, earthy colors and textures to outdoor rooms. Perhaps because of their natural tones, these fired clay tiles seem at home with a wide range of house styles. Hand-made terra cotta tiles have a rustic beauty that suits traditional patios and courtyards, but their rather soft, porous composition makes them unsuitable for cold- or wet-weather applications. By contrast, most manufactured tiles are impervious to water and have a strength and durability that tolerate a variety of outdoor conditions, including frost. Unglazed versions with matte or gritty surfaces aren't as slippery when the surface is damp or wet. Machine-formed terra cotta tiles, both domestic and imported, are available in an impressive array of patterns, colors, and textures that can evoke images of ancient Rome or complement even the most contemporary architectural design.

One of the oldest building and paving materials known to man, ceramic tile proves to be a substantial, practical, and beautiful choice by today's standards as well.

WARM TEXTURES

This small-scale patio (right) gets much of its old-world charm from simple materials. Wide grout lines that mask uneven edges and mottled colors give the tiles a hand-crafted look. Outdoor furniture: Brown Jordan Company.

INVITING BACKDROP

A hand-painted wall mural of flowering vines adds to the light mood of this canopied veranda (below). The ceramic tile floor carries warm colors that blend harmoniously with the cool blues of the comfortable wicker furnishings. Wall tile: Summitville Tiles, Inc. Tile: Ceramica Mayor, S.A./Villar Tile, Inc. Tile inserts: Seneca Tiles, Inc. Patio furniture: Patio Plus.

CONTINUOUS BEAUTY

A new surface of terra cotta tile transformed this once drab concrete patio (above) into a warm, inviting poolside surround. Blue tile inserts carry the pool color across the patio. Tile design: Jonna Avella Designs. Tile: Ceramica Mayor, S.A./Villar Tile, Inc. Tile inserts: Seneca Tiles, Inc.

CONTRASTS FOR SPECIAL EFFECTS

SPLENDID RESULTS

Bands of cheerful blue tile enliven a corner of this patio (left) and break up the concrete surface with a splash of color. Red brick coping, shredded bark, and a border of greenery introduce other color and material contrasts. Design: Peridian International.

Sometimes the most visually satisfying patios result from the juxtaposition of contrasting materials or from unexpected combinations of similar ones. The effects can be subtle or stimulating, depending on the mixture and the medium. A patio laid primarily in rectangular-cut flagstones can seem a little less formal with smaller pieces of contrasting stone placed here and there or grouped in a border. A dark brick patio edged with white crushed stone appears crisp and tailored. A light concrete surface accented with bright tile stripes takes on visual punch. Contrasting colors and textures are especially effective in bringing plain masonry to life and drawing the eye away from potentially monotonous surfaces.

Special effects can be achieved through pattern, too. And although brick is the material most often associated with pattern, concrete pavers, cut stone, tile, and small smooth rocks all lend themselves to unusual—even elaborate—designs.

LUMINOUS PATTERN

This enclosed patio (left) pairs traditional flagstone with contemporary glass block in an intriguing design. The contrasting colored glass blocks carry a special layered coating that reflects light. Brick: Acme Brick Company.

CUSTOM MATCH

This tailored entry walkway (above) blends poured concrete with redwood strips and a brick border in a neat geometric design. The dividers add interest and create joints that help prevent cracks in the concrete slab.

MIX AND MATCH MATERIALS

While contrasting materials are often employed to solve problems or create dramatic effects, they can also be mixed and matched just to add a little visual interest to an informal outdoor area. The combinations can be as straightforward as brick and concrete block laid in sand or wood strips neatly edging a gravel walkway. Materials might contrast in texture but wear colors bearing a close resemblance to each other; or they might differ in color but carry a similar size, shape, and surface. The emphasis might be on blending materials into a pattern. Simple patterns such as a grid or checkerboard lend themselves to casual patio styles and can be easily accomplished with any square or rectangular paving material.

Whether mixing materials for informal looks or to create a more striking patio, it's wise to gather a small assortment of the pavings in advance and lay out a sample section of the area to be certain that they blend together in functional and visually pleasing ways.

INFORMAL PAIRING

This festive, cozy patio (right) combines premolded concrete block with standard brick in a lively, unpretentious pattern. Although the colors set up contrasts, the materials have similar surface textures. Clear protective coating: Thompson's Water Seal.

DRAMATIC COMBINATION

Large stone tiles and smaller stones cut in a Belgian block shape work comfortably together on this restful patio (above). The cool grayish tints of the patio floor harmonize beautifully with the light wood tones of the vine-draped pergola and low planters. Pergola design: Robert Orr and Melanie Taylor.

VERSATILE POURED CONCRETE

Strong, serviceable poured concrete is a surprisingly versatile paving material. One of its most respected qualities is the ability to take to nearly any shape or style—large or small, formal or casual. And because it is a molded material—placed into a prepared form of some type and allowed to harden—concrete can conform to a wide spectrum of landscape and patio designs and suit a number of architectural styles. Concrete can be made to flow freely around the perimeter of a house, following its contours closely and serving as a continuous surface that might incorporate steps, planters, and walls into the patio plan. Or it can be molded into a series of separate but related patio elements, each cast in individual forms that can be different in size and shape or all the same. One advantage of working with smaller sections of concrete is that other materials can be integrated rather easily to introduce variety. Poured concrete can also function successfully as an accent, perhaps as stepping stones linking the house to the garden or low benches surrounding a small pond.

GRAND ACCENTS

Like giant lily pads, these free-form concrete stepping stones (left) seem to float across the lawn. Their whimsical appearance contrasts pleasantly with the rather formal attitude of the house and its plantings. Design: Rodney Stutman. Landscape design: Nick Williams.

ELEGANT SETTING

Scored to resemble big stone tiles, this basic concrete floor (left) serves as a cool, understated backdrop for the warm-climate mood of this sheltered outdoor living space. The ornate but airy furnishings inject a Mediterranean note. Patio doors: Eagle Window & Door Co.

DISGUISING BASIC CONCRETE

As a reliable, practical, and economical paving for patios and walkways, concrete performs admirably on its own. But it can gain dramatically in its overall appeal when given a decorative finish that banishes any visual sensation of cold, drab, or bland.

Color, for instance, can do wonders to cheer up basic concrete. The pigment can be mixed into the material before it's poured for a lasting, color-through finish, or it can be dusted onto a leveled, wet surface and smoothed in with a trowel. Sometimes concrete gets its color after it has hardened from an application of paint or a penetrating stain.

Basic concrete can also benefit from a variety of textured effects, from simple broomed and salt-pocked finishes to imprinted surfaces that disguise a slab as brick, tile, or natural stone. Although small areas of concrete take to imprinting, or stamping, with tools that can be rented from a home improvement center, large expanses usually require the skills and equipment of a professional contractor to ensure realistic-looking results.

TOUCH OF CLASS

This handsome treatment of basic concrete (above) banishes any notion of a drab or bland material. Bordered by a crisp smooth band of white concrete, the imprinted areas of the walkway and terrace resemble cut flagstone laid in a rectangular pattern. Patio construction: KD Fencing, Ltd.

RUSTIC APPEAL

Tucked snugly against the house, this inviting rear patio (right) carries a stamped concrete finish with the look and feel of terra cotta tile. Its rustic, antiqued appearance suggests traditional hand-made pavers. Patio design and construction: KD Fencing, Ltd.

REALISTIC TRANSFORMATION

An island in a sea of green lawn, this free-form concrete slab is cleverly disguised as a natural stone patio (above). Its soft colors and slightly roughened surface harmonize gracefully with the naturalistic landscape of rugged boulders and low shrubs. Patio design and construction: KD Fencing, Ltd.

CONCRETE TAKES A CREATIVE PATH

This breezy informal patio and walkway (below) feature a stamped concrete finish that echoes the colors and mood of the oceanside setting. As the bold design of the concrete walkway follows the path to the water, it teases the eye with patterns that evoke a variety of images. Concrete design: Bomanite Corp.

Distinctive in appearance, innovative in design, and completely functional, imprinted cast-in-place concrete is showing up in more and more patios and walkways. Innovative techniques for integrating color and embossing the surface are resulting in more realistic-looking finishes and an expanded selection of patterns. Familiar flagstone and Belgian block designs, for instance, are being joined by a number of other creative finishes: used brick laid in a variety of patterns, Moorish-look tile, granite in a fishscale design, wood planks, and even fancy borders and upbeat graphics with 3-D effects. With so many options, concrete is no longer regarded as a practical-but-plain paving alternative.

Because of the wealth of decorative finishes to select from, imprinted concrete can be easily tailored to suit virtually any house style. It can be combined with other masonry materials to achieve a particular mood and create visual interest. And, thanks to its molded character, it can be physically shaped to integrate with the existing landscape or complement a new design.

A graceful border of bright marigolds accompanies this concrete walkway (right) on its route to the porch. The subdued earth colors and stone tile appearance of the imprinted surface blend smoothly with the brick and wood materials of the traditionally styled house. Concrete design: Bomanite Corp.

FEATURE ATTRACTIONS

A basic patio can function adequately and attractively with a little dressing up, using items such as a dining table and chairs or some colorful potted plants. But a patio can get a lot more use with the addition of a few custom elements. Introducing a water feature might be one route to take. While incorporating a swimming pool into a patio design is usually a major project, especially if the patio is already in place, its rewards can be worth the effort. A spa can be easily integrated into an existing design and may offer just as much relaxation as a full-fledged swimming pool. Water can be an attraction in a purely decorative form, too, consisting of a simple plant-filled pond, an elegant splashing fountain, or a quiet reflecting pool.

Much like decks, patios lend themselves to a variety of built-in features. Thanks to their masonry materials, brick and stone barbecues are a popular patio attraction and have a safety advantage over barbecues on or near wood decks. Stairs may be an essential component, but they also serve as a visual transition from one place to another. Finally, built-in seating and planters can add the finishing touches to a patio or garden design.

HARMONIOUS FEATURES

This inviting patio (right) brings several functional and decorative attractions to its garden setting. The curving pool, bubbling spa, and rock-formed waterfall work well together, featuring water as the focal point. The informal pool house offers a shady place to enjoy a cool drink and a snack. Concrete design: Bomanite Corp.

INVIGORATING FOCAL POINTS

Without a doubt, swimming pools are one of the most popular and dominant patio features. Their presence adds value to the home, gives focus to the patio and nearby areas, and provides hours of enjoyment for both serious swimmers and casual bathers. The neat, orderly shape of rectangular pools usually lends a formality to patio settings that suits both traditional and contemporary house styles. When contoured into free-form shapes, pools have a more casual look, especially when surrounded by natural landscaping. Poolside paving materials can be as varied as the patio designs themselves. Brick, flagstone, and textured concrete—aggregate and imprinted concrete in particular—are among the favorites. Though highly attractive, ceramic tile is usually too slippery a surface to use around water.

Because of their visual dominance, swimming pools and their patio surrounds should be sized to harmonize with the scale and proportions of the house, especially if they lie in close proximity. It's also a good idea to situate the pool where it can get plenty of sun, a little shade, and some protection from the wind.

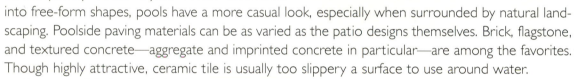

MAIN ATTRACTION

In perfect balance with the size and scale of the house and patio, this lap pool (above) carries a crisp elegance that suits the traditional setting. Hand-cut flagstone—this variety is called bluestone—paves both the patio and the pool surround. Pool construction: Rizzo Construction Pool Company, Inc.

CREATIVE DESIGN

Modern forms and materials characterize this arresting contemporary desert home (left). A challenge to construct, the pool was built on a 22-degree bedrock slope and required a hefty substructure of piers and retaining walls for support. The pool decking is surfaced in exposed aggregate, while stairways carry Mexican terra cotta tiles. Pool construction: Pioneer Pools.

OUTDOOR ENJOYMENT

A sculptural free-form pool serves as the dramatic focal point of this expansive multiterraced patio design (right). The textured concrete floor, colored and imprinted to resemble tile, is a perfect complement to the Mediterranean-style house and its garden accents. Concrete design: Bomanite Corp.

SPA-SOAKING ON THE PATIO

As an amenity to the patio, spas rank high in bringing pleasure to outdoor living, whether enjoyed as a private spot for relaxing or a gathering place for social events. Though often included as an integral component of a swimming pool design, a spa can also work well as a stand-alone feature that functions beautifully in a small space. In fact, part of a spa's attraction is its ability to tuck into a little corner off the master bedroom or to fit into a narrow side patio alongside the family room. Regardless of its location, though, any spa should have convenient access to the house with some kind of visual screening from the street and close neighbors.

When integrated into a pool design, the top of the spa might be flush with the pool surround, as is typical in wood decks. Most freestanding spas, however, rest on a stable sand or soil base—as does the patio itself—and are elevated, hot-tub style. This prominent position above the floor provides wonderful opportunities to dress up spa walls and the rim with decorative stonework and fancy tiles to create a dramatic focal point.

POINT OF INTEREST

Creative design, attention to detail, and architectural drama set this pool and patio area (left) apart as a true showpiece. A three-tiered waterfall gracefully flows from the house to the free-form swimming pool, which features a handsome spa.

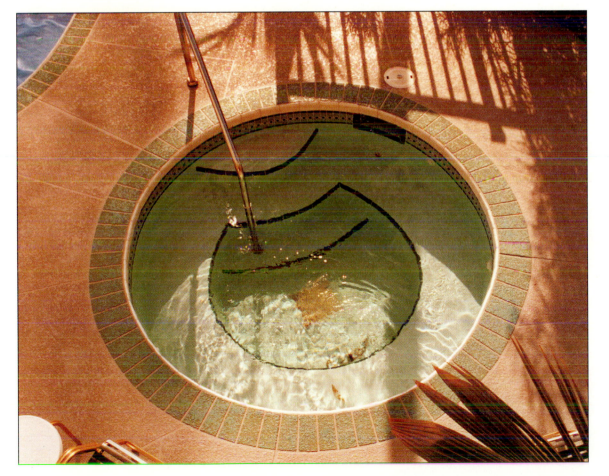

FINISHING TOUCH

The tile-look border around this poolside spa (left) is really a spray-on decorative overlay that dresses up basic concrete with color, pattern, and texture. Together, the outer border and inner ring of tiles give the spa an Art Deco look.
Spray-on overlay: Inco Chemical Supply Company, Inc.

SOOTHING SIGHTS AND SOUNDS

Flowing or still, a water feature such as a pond or pool brings a feeling of serenity to a garden or patio. It might be a central focus, positioned so that indoor and outdoor areas can enjoy its sights and sounds, or it might be nestled in a secluded corner that encourages quiet contemplation. Without the agitation of a waterfall or fountain, reflecting pools are still waters of tranquility designed to mirror the natural surroundings—branching tree limbs, for example, or even clouds sailing across the sky. Many pools, however, incorporate waterfalls for the simple beauty that moving water can bring to a setting. Most ponds are planned with aquatic plants in mind and should be placed where there is sun for at least some of the day. When fish are to be included, care must be taken to provide a healthy and balanced environment for both plants and animals.

Water features can take on formal or informal looks. A rectangular pool edged with flagstone or brick has a formal appearance, but it can be softened with the colors and textures of items such as water lilies, a border of natural stones, or low plantings. Curving pools seem less formal and are especially attractive when integrated with a rock garden.

STILL WATERS

This small free-form pool (above) tucked in a corner of the patio proves even a cozy outdoor area can be home to a water attraction. Pool system: Lilypons Water Gardens.

BEAUTY IN MOTION

A perfect complement to informal waterscapes, a rock garden lends color and texture to this pool's (right) naturalistic design. The waterfall adds a soothing, refreshing note to the area.

TRANQUIL SETTING

A variety of aquatic plants and a careful arrangement of rustic stones soften the rather formal mood of this inviting design (left). The flagstone ledge edging the pool makes a fine seat for pausing to enjoy the water on the journey through the garden. Pool system: Lilypons Water Gardens.

This naturalistic swimming pool (left) features water in motion. The earthy Sedona red flagstone paving this area and the patio sets up a vibrant contrast with the black glass veneer and granite lining the pool walls and floor. Design: Skip Phillips.

WATER IN MOTION

As decorative accents, fountains and waterfalls can make any water feature more vibrant and alive, and when they are lit by night, they can bring spectacular looks to a patio or garden. Whether they arc out, spray up, or spill over, fountains are nearly always a focal point. Their splashing sounds attract attention, too, and serve to muffle unwanted noises. Fountains and waterfalls tend to bring a bit of formality to an outdoor area since they are so distinct from the natural landscape. A pool with a fountain is an especially pleasant addition to an entry patio or courtyard, giving visitors an elegant greeting. Even a tiny patio, too small for a pool of any size, can enjoy water in motion with a low-profile fountain mounted on the wall. Waterfalls in a patio setting typically have a gentler presence than fountains, flowing over rocks or masonry in a meandering, informal path.

Incorporating a water feature into a patio requires thoughtful planning. Fountains and waterfalls, for instance, require pumps and controls, which may be one reason they are often integrated with swimming pool systems.

Beautifully balanced in symmetry and line, this handsome swimming pool (left) features a triple fountain enclosed by a glass block wall. The sculptural surround ringing the area is paved in embossed, colored concrete. Concrete design: Bomanite Corp.

CLASSIC BUILT-IN BARBECUES

Well-designed, well-built masonry barbecues bring permanent good looks to a patio and can provide years of service for outdoor entertaining. Brick stands out as the classic masonry material for barbecues due to its convenient shape and size and its traditional role in fireplace design. But concrete construction is also a reliable alternative and can be most attractive when faced with tile or stone. A masonry barbecue can be fashioned to accommodate a variety of cooking preferences, from old-fashioned fireplace/ovens that grill foods over an open charcoal or wood flame, to covered kettle-style cookers for roasting or smoking, to up-to-the-minute gas-fired and electric units that behave much like a standard indoor oven.

Whatever the building material or the cooking style, it's a good idea to include some counter space and storage areas in the barbecue design or somewhere nearby. And if there's plenty of patio space to spare for a large, well-appointed barbecue area, consider incorporating a serving buffet, a sink, and perhaps even an undercounter refrigerator. These amenities can go a long way to transform an ordinary outdoor cooking experience into a memorable event.

DETAILS THAT MAKE A DIFFERENCE

The eye-pleasing brickwork of this combination fireplace and barbecue (left) is set off handsomely by a lattice privacy screen, matching planters, and an overhead structure of wood timbers bearing a Craftsman touch. Rustic wood counters flanking the barbecue and a shelf above provide handy places to put dishes down and to serve food.

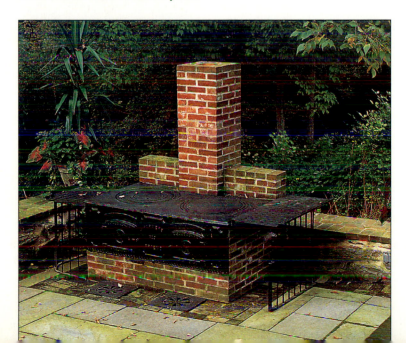

GREAT BARBECUES

This sunken barbecue area (left) was planned for serious cooking. The wood-burning cast-iron ovens feature a large surface that can heat up an ample quantity of food and keep it all warm. The stone wall edging the patio creates convenient seating for dining informally or just socializing.

EASY TO MAINTAIN

A colorful focal point at the edge of the patio, this barbecue island (below) carries a cobalt blue tile work surface and Mediterranean-inspired, blue- and white-patterned tiles on its face and sides. Decorative and practical, ceramic tiles are a breeze to keep clean. Tile: Grespania, S.A.

SEATING AS A GARDEN ACCENT

Few patios can function well or host outdoor activities without some kind of seating. Sometimes seating serves as a dominant feature or even the focal point, as might a large grouping of furnishings. It often acts as an accent to draw attention to a particular area such as a fragrant flower garden or a lovely view. Freestanding or built-in, accent seating can offer a place to rest after a brisk walk, take a break from yard work, or settle down with a good book.

Seating for the patio comes in many styles and materials that can suit a variety of settings. Benches, wood or stone, seem particularly at home both on the patio and in the garden. English-style teakwood benches can be pleasing additions to traditional designs, especially when the wood has acquired a silvery patina with time and weather. Stone and cast concrete benches have rustic appeal, but they can be uncomfortable for long-term sitting unless cushioned or outfitted with a wood surface. Park benches, with their slatted wood seats and backrests and metal arms and legs, can adapt to many outdoor areas and look especially festive when brightly painted.

RUSTIC APPEAL

Nestled into a plant-protected corner of the patio, this weathered wood bench (left) rests atop a permanent masonry base. The carved backrest and arms add simple beauty to the somewhat plain design.

NATURAL SEATING

Recessed into the hillside, this rustic stone bench (above) melds unobtrusively into the landscape. The large flat stones of the seat and backpiece harmonize with the randomly laid stonework of the patio floor.

DECORATIVE FEATURE

Shaped to follow the curving contours of the cut stone wall, this inviting garden bench (above) provides enough room for several people to sit amid colorful surroundings.

STAIRS RISE TO THE OCCASION

The chunky, rough-cut concrete blocks edging these patio steps (below) provide an interesting textural contrast to the uniform, bricklike shape of the pavers on the floor.

Stairs are essential ingredients in many patio designs, but they can also rise to the occasion as decorative features that tie various elements together. Stairs can be fashioned out of the same paving material as the patio floor but take on added interest with a different texture or pattern, such as a poured concrete surface changing to rougher concrete block or brick laid in a herringbone pattern changing to a straight run. Stairs often look their best when their design combines the primary patio material with a contrasting one, such as exposed aggregate teamed with wood or brick accents or large formal flagstones softened with a random arrangement of small smooth-surface rocks.

Changing the width and depth of stairs can create interesting effects, too. Vertical risers should remain a uniform height for safety when climbing or descending, but the proportions of horizontal treads—the walking surface—can be varied with great flexibility. Stairs might broaden as they lead from the patio adjoining the house down to another area of the yard. Or a short flight of standard-depth stairs might open to a series of platformlike levels for a terraced appearance.

A grouping of clay pots bearing a profusion of flowers escorts walkers on their climb up the unglazed terra cotta tile stairs (right). Stuccoed planters, also brimming with flowers, help give the area a sheltered, intimate feeling.